SIOP

Books by Peter Pringle

INSIGHT ON THE MIDDLE EAST WAR
(with Sunday Times *Insight Team)*

YEAR OF THE CAPTAINS: AN ACCOUNT OF THE
PORTUGUESE REVOLUTION
(with Sunday Times *Insight Team)*

THE NUCLEAR BARONS
(with James Spigelman)

Books by William Arkin

RESEARCH GUIDE TO CURRENT MILITARY AND
STRATEGIC AFFAIRS

NUCLEAR WEAPONS DATA BOOK
(with Thomas Cochran)

SIOP
The Secret U.S. Plan
for Nuclear War

PETER PRINGLE
and
WILLIAM ARKIN

W.W. NORTON & COMPANY
New York London

The text of this book is composed in 11/14 Gael, with
display type set in Craw Modern. Composition and
manufacturing by The Haddon Craftsmen, Inc.
Book design by Nancy Dale Muldoon

First Edition

Library of Congress Cataloging in Publication Data

Pringle, Peter.
SIOP, the secret U.S. plan for nuclear war.

Bibliography: p.
Includes index.
1. Atomic warfare.   2. Military planning—United
States.   3. United states—Military policy. I. Arkin,
William M.   II. Title.   III. Title: S.I.O.P., the
secret U.S. plan for nuclear war.
U263.P74 1983   355'.0217   83–6801

ISBN 0-393-01798-2

W. W. Norton & Company, Inc., 500 Fifth Avenue, New York, N. Y. 10110
W. W. Norton & Company Ltd., 37 Great Russell Street, London WC1B 3NU

1 2 3 4 5 6 7 8 9 0

"The tremendous multiplication of destructive power that the atomic bomb gives to aircraft, together with the constant shrinkage the globe is undergoing with each increase in the ranges and speeds of aircraft, lends an urgency to the solution of the defense problem that the United States has never before known in time of peace."

Report of the U.S. Air Force, 30 June 1948

Contents

Acknowledgments

IN writing this account, we owe a great deal to many people who have been generous with their time and their experience. We owe special gratitude to Desmond Ball, John Bierman, Bruce Blair, John Bohn, John Bradley, Duncan Campbell, Jane Cousins, Daniel Ellsberg, Richard Fieldhouse, Barry Horowitz, Ted Jarvis, Michal Levin, Robert S. Norris, Michael del Papa, Christopher Paine, Gwyn Prins, George Rathjens, John Ritch, Jack Ruina, David Rosenberg, Pete Scoville, William Shawcross, John Steinbrunner, Ed Ulsamer, and Mary Warren.

We thank the staffs of many U.S. Public Affairs Departments, Freedom of Information Act officers and official historians at the Defense Department, Air Force Headquarters, Defense Communications Agency, Electronic Systems Division, Air Force Communications Command, Army Communications Command, Naval Telecommunications Command, Strategic Air Command, and North American Aerospace Defense Command. One reasonable request seemed unreasonably refused: a tour of the National Military Command Center. The librarians at the Pentagon were very patient with a stream of requests. The staff of the Foreign Press Center in Washington, D.C., especially Lieutenant Commander Jolene Keefer, helped to arrange visits and interviews, and the U.S. Air Force 5th Bombardment Wing, Heavy, graciously squeezed us into their exacting schedule at Minot Air Force Base, North Dakota.

We would each like to extend thanks to our respective colleagues at the *Observer* and the Institute for Policy Studies in Washington, especially Robert Chesshyre, Helen Friedman, and Richard Fieldhouse, who bore the brunt of our own heavy schedules while this book was being written.

The manuscript was read by Eleanor Randolph, who improved it enormously, particularly by making us demystify the obscure jargon of nuclear weapons and military strategy.

Finally, we thank our New York agent, Robert Ducas, and at W. W. Norton our editor, Starling Lawrence, and our copy editor, Debra Makay, for involving themselves personally in turning the manuscript into a book.

Preface

THE title of this book is a strange and unfamiliar acronym for the plan the United States has been working on since 1960 to wage a nuclear war with the Soviet Union. SIOP stands for Single Integrated Operational Plan—single because it is the only contingency plan that accounts for the nuclear weapons of all three branches of the United States military, and integrated because it embraces all the nuclear contingency plans of the United States' regional commands in the Pacific, the Atlantic, and Europe, plus the lesser forces of America's closest and only real nuclear ally, Britain.

The SIOP is the central and most secret part of the West's nuclear deterrent. In fact, the SIOP is so secret that it has its own security classification: Extremely Sensitive Information, or ESI. Until recently, the letters S-I-O-P rarely appeared in the mountain of public documents and strategic analyses that have flowed from the Pentagon and the private institutions where the policies of the nuclear age are conceived and studied. When we told a U.S.

Air Force officer, in the spring of 1982, that we were writing a book about the SIOP, he turned to a colleague; "Did you hear that?" he asked incredulously. Then, turning to us, he said, "How can you possibly find out enough information about the SIOP to write a book?"

Here is our answer. Despite a concerted effort by government and military groups over the years to restrict access to information about nuclear weapons, legal mechanisms in the United States such as the Freedom of Information Act and the mandatory thirty-year declassification rule have begun to close significant gaps in our nuclear history. The intensive efforts of a small coterie of military researchers, professional historians, journalists, and ordinary citizens engaged in a healthy ongoing debate about nuclear weapons have helped to peel back some of the layers of unnecessary secrecy. A better picture of high-level decisions and policymaking on the matter of nuclear war has finally started to emerge.

Dealing with the SIOP has not been an easy task, but we discovered that an extraordinary amount of information is available in the public record, not just about the war plan and its history, but also about its huge support systems of command posts, communications links, and intelligence collection. We were also surprised how much of this system was open to public view. Many of the dedicated and well-intentioned men and women who work with the war plans, and would execute the SIOP in time of war, are willing, able, and sometimes even eager to talk about their trade. Military people often feel they are misunderstood, that their work is not appreciated because the public doesn't fully understand what they do and how they do it. But if that is true for most military groups, it is even more so for the practitioners of nuclear war planning. Their craft was conceived in the utmost secrecy after World War II, and people have been so conditioned by the past that merely to ask what has been going on is considered by many a "seditious" act.

Key parts of the system can be revealed and explained without jeopardizing national security, however, and on a tour of the missile early-warning sites and command posts we were taken behind doors bearing signs warning that illegal entry would be met with "deadly force" and shown the war rooms where the generals would sit and direct their nuclear forces. At the headquarters of Strategic Air Command in Omaha, Nebraska, we were shown the red metal boxes, secured with padlocks, where the war codes and plans are kept. The duty officers interrupted their constant vigil of distant horizons to explain how the plan would be used and they ran mock tapes of a simulated Soviet attack through the computers. They told us the special code words for missile launches and which "hot lines" would be used by whom in the execution of nuclear war. They took us up in their aging B–52 bombers and, from a height of only 400 feet, we flew under the "enemy" radar and "bombed" Utah and Nevada with nuclear weapons. They took us down within a Minuteman missile silo, and the young air force officers who would "turn the key" to send the missile on its way to the Soviet Union gave the chilling, time-honored reply to our question Don't you ever think about where the missile is going?—"It makes no difference to us, sir," one said, "our job is to launch them."

On the New England coast, members of the U.S. Air Force gave us a tour of their latest early warning device, a prize radar that can detect a submarine-launched missile anywhere in the North Atlantic. If this remarkable machine ever spots an incoming Soviet missile, it automatically computes the missiles's trajectory and speed into an estimated time of arrival over its American target. While this is indeed a wonder of technology, one cannot help thinking, What's the point? The missile may take only a few minutes, perhaps less than eight, to reach its target. Can the president of the United States get the information in time to decide what to do? Suppose he is out horseback riding, or giving a speech on television, or sleeping off a state dinner? The air force has a special communications system that will alert the president immediately, wherever he may be, about an attack and give him a scant moment to reflect before he must respond. The question is whether the president and his military aides would be able to make a rational and responsible decision in such a short time and under any of a vast variety of circumstances. This is one of the most important unknowns in the complex world of nuclear possibilities, and one that we explore many times throughout this book. Considering all the elaborate plans in existence for waging nuclear war with the Soviet Union, would the president ever have time, in a crisis, to do anything other than what the generals told him to do? Has the SIOP become a mere symbol of presidential control over nuclear weapons that, in reality, no longer exists?

During our conversations with war planners and nuclear strategists and in our own independent researches, we found, and had to identify, many strange acronyms that form the key parts of the SIOP. They are used not merely to confuse outsiders but to create the aura of a private club that deals in secret information and speaks in riddles and passwords. Finding out what these people do, decoding the acronyms, and understanding the organizations and plans they represent are the first step to a real understanding of the nuclear arms race. What drove America's stockpile of nuclear weapons ever upward from 2 in 1945 to 32,000 in 1967—and even higher still in the coming decade? Has the West's policy of nuclear deterrence been enhanced by increasing the SIOP target list from a few hundred to today's 40,000? If the West spends billions of dollars on communications equipment and command bunkers in preparation to fight a nuclear war will the world be a safer place, or will the preparation and readiness more likely cause a nuclear war?

This book is the first comprehensive inquiry into the SIOP and its supporting system of command posts that run the West's nuclear forces. It traces the changing makeup of the SIOP through the days of Eisenhower's massive retaliation doctrine, MacNamara's mutual assured destruction (MAD), Nixon's controlled responses, Carter's countervailing strategy, and, finally, to Ronald Reagan's alarming concept of nuclear victories. By way of introduction to the many facets of the SIOP we begin with an actual nuclear war game played by the Reagan administration in the spring of 1982. The results of this game, like the results of all nuclear war games, are classified Top Secret, but for reasons that will become clear later, several of the key details have leaked to the public. By using those reports and unclassified Pentagon regulations governing the waging of nuclear war, we have reconstructed how the generals and the White House might have played the game, that is, what messages they sent to each other and what decisions were made and why.

The game, the largest of its kind ever played by United States forces, begins with one of the standard doomsday scenarios in the Pentagon's repertoire: an attack on South Korea by North Korean troops. But the purpose of this game is not to see if a defense can be mounted and nuclear war avoided; rather, the game assumes that the participants will begin using nuclear weapons almost immediately. The generals, sitting in their bunkers far away from the front lines, succeed in this game if they and their command posts survive the first nuclear strikes and the lines of communications between them and their nuclear forces remain open. The generals must be able to use these communications to order a nuclear response and, at the same time, restore a tattered United States government and the remnants of its Western society to some semblance of a working order.

In the end, the game begs the central question about our modern nuclear strategy: Has the nuclear age evolved to a point where the generals and the politicians feel confident enough about controlling a nuclear war and its aftermath that nuclear weapons might now be used? Today's nuclear posturing in the Western Alliance includes a troubling inconsistency. On the one hand, the objective is still the same as it was in Harry Truman's day, namely, to rid the planet of all nuclear weapons. On the other hand, the Pentagon is asking for billions of dollars to upgrade their command posts and their communication links so that they can actually use their nuclear weapons in battle. But what do they really want? The key to unraveling the inconsistency is the Single Integrated Op-

erational Plan; this is the document that distinguishes between political rhetoric and military realities. It is the
only document in the Pentagon that can really tell us how
close we have come to nuclear war.

Peter Pringle and William Arkin
Washington, D.C., June 1983

SIOP

1
Cocked Pistol

LONG before microwave communications and the satellite age, conquering generals knew that military strategy was only half the battle. If they could not keep in touch with their men there was no point in having a war plan. Yet the modern planners of nuclear war have tended to forget such things. The surrogate wars they have plotted on their computers and wall charts have concentrated on the massive destructive power of the weapons themselves—which side has the most nuclear warheads and which side could deliver them in the best way, either with missiles by land or by sea, or from fleets of long-range bombers. Their mock battles have been short and decisive, involving the leveling of the enemy's territory and decimating its population. War games have ended, and winners have been declared, according to how many enemy targets were obliterated. But today, the age of the prolonged nuclear war is replacing the spasm "all-in-one-go" scenarios of yesteryear. The war games that generals are playing today test how commanders would order the use of nuclear weapons; they are about the telephones, the radio links, the satellites, and the computers that would be used to transmit orders to fight the big war. These "games" test whether the president is able to communicate with his nuclear forces during and after an attack and, most important, they examine the ability of the president and his generals to survive long enough in their command bunkers to continue ordering the nuclear forces into action during an extended nuclear war.

On 1 March 1982, the United States began such a war game in total secrecy. Given the innocent-sounding code name, Ivy League, this game was no demonstration of military might or even computerized sport. Ivy League was the biggest command-post exercise in thirty years, an intensive five-day exercise that alerted troops around the globe and used high-ranking civilian officials as stand-ins for the president and his battery of top aides. In the end it marked a turning point in American nuclear strategy, because at the close of Day 5 commanders had survived long enough in their underground bunkers to fight a drawn-out nuclear war with the Soviet Union. Although the specific results of this game remain classified, it is possible to piece together an account of how it was played. The "cards" in this contest are the military messages, some routine and some top secret, that come into the command centers in Washington, D.C., from all over the world. These messages have been reconstructed using the Pentagon's own unclassified signals handbooks, and they appear in the same format as the Pentagon used in its latest version of World War III. The actual sites where the action took place and the general course of the "war" have been made public.

Ivy League 82 opens in Hawaii on the afternoon of 1
March 1983.*

*"This is an OPREP-3 from 3rd Brigade Operations Center,
2nd Infantry Division. Radar Site 5 reported at 011345Z
unusual unidentified military movement including infantry and truck activity at CT10511256. It appears that the
activity is taking place in the DMZ. Aerial reconnaissance
has been requested. Additional report will follow."*
The first message came routinely, by telephone. The
voice from Korea told the duty officer in the Emergency
Operations Center of the U.S. Pacific Command (PACOM)
in Hawaii that there had been unusual troop movement in
the sensitive no man's land between North and South
Korea, something that happens with monotonous regular-
ity. The message came bearing the code word OPREP, for
operations report, and the number 3. This meant that the
incident could have "political ramifications," but scores
of such messages are sent every day throughout the U.S.
armed forces and cover anything from a barroom brawl
to a full-blown diplomatic incident. This message, however, was only the beginning of many that would eventually put the entire U.S. military, including its commander
in chief, the president, in the highest state of readiness for
a mock nuclear war. It was the first stirring of a mock
battle that would be played out in secret underground
command centers, on highly sophisticated communications networks, on videoscreens and computer terminals,
and, finally, in the president's "doomsday" plane that sits

---

*All messages in the reconstruction of Ivy League have been compiled by the
authors from available data, and the troop movements represent simulations of
those made during the exercise.

*hauntingly on the tarmac at Andrews Air Force Base near
Washington, D.C., waiting to spirit the nation's remaining
leaders away from the nuclear fray.*

*Ivy League began slowly. The first report had come
from Korea at 1:45 in the afternoon and was followed, two
hours and seven minutes later, by a second report from a
U.S. unit called the Tunnel Neutralization Team that is
charged with the bizarre mission of detecting North Korean tunnels underneath the two and a half mile DMZ.
Three tunnels have been discovered in the last eight
years; the longest, uncovered in 1978, stretched a mile
through solid granite under South Korean territory, an
underground byway large enough to drive a truck through.
Few analysts take the tunnels seriously as a possible
invasion route, but the detection team reported they had
heard odd sounds below ground.*

*In the next six hours American troops throughout Korea
began reporting military activity in the DMZ and elsewhere, including two North Korean commando boats
south of the DMZ off Taebu-do Island. At the same time,
intelligence information of unusual Warsaw Pact troop
movements in Europe and elsewhere began to flow into
Washington. These reports, previously unclassified, now
carried a SECRET stamp. Moreover, a code word, PINNACLE,
began appearing on the messages: It meant they were now
bypassing the regional commanders and being sent directly to the Joint Chiefs of Staff and, ultimately, to the
president himself.*

*The messages were buzzing through secure lines into
three command centers on the American continent. They
were moved simultaneously to the White House Situation
Room, a windowless sub-basement chamber under the*

Oval Office; to the National Military Command Center, a series of office suites on the third floor of the Pentagon; and to the backup command post, known as the Alternate National Military Command Center, deep inside Raven Rock Mountain in southern Pennsylvania.

The center of activity was the command post in the Pentagon where, at 10 P.M. on the first day, the Joint Chiefs and their aides were roused from their comfortable suburban homes around Washington, D.C., and whisked by chauffeur-driven cars to the briefing chamber on the third floor. Next to an office full of clattering telex machines, a bank of clocks set for a variety of world time zones, and a spread of maps showing the dispersal of troops, both East and West, the generals gathered in the emergency conference room, strangely quiet by comparison. The duty officers, known as the "battle staff," sit at a huge T-shaped table and four Emergency Action Officers concentrate on built-in consoles linking them to American forces worldwide.

The Joint Chiefs, perched on a platform slightly above the battle staff, listened to the briefing officers gauge the seriousness of the latest messages from Korea. On six huge, color display screens flashing world maps, charts, photographs, and troop concentrations, the battle staff laid out the possibilities from the single distant act in the DMZ. The signs were not good: The last message received from Korea showed that the North Koreans had started a massive invasion of the South. Troops, tanks, and heavy equipment were streaming over the border half a world away.

The course of the war was being monitored from several places at once. Identical batteries of communications

equipment at the White House and at the alternate com-
mand post in Pennsylvania formed part of the vast net-
work of telephones and telex machines tied by satellite,
radio, and computers. The Joint Chiefs made their next
move from the so-called Gold Room, another conference
suite on the third-floor Pentagon complex. Together with
the secretary of defense and with the approval of the
president, they decided to upgrade the alert status of the
U.S. forces. Known as Defense Readiness Conditions, or
DEFCONS, the alerts range from 5 to 1 with 1 being the
ultimate state of emergency or "maximum force readi-
ness." The Joint Chiefs put most U.S. forces on DEFCON-4,
but the troops in the Pacific region went to DEFCON-3. The
next day the forces were put on DEFCON-1, appropriately
code named Cocked Pistol. At the end of the first day, the
defense secretary's message read as follows (The "S" in
parentheses means it was stamped SECRET):

    FLASH OVERRIDE
      FROM: JCS WASHINGTON DC//J3 NMCC//
      TO: AIG 931
      AIG 6861
      SECRET
      FJ045//001//012335Z MAR 82//

    (S) SECRETARY OF DEFENSE HAS DECLARED STEP UP
IN DEFENSE READINESS CONDITIONS (DEFCON) FROM
NORMAL READINESS (DEFCON 5) FOR US FORCES
WORLDWIDE TO DEFCON 4 AND FROM DEFCON 4 FOR
PACIFIC COMMAND FORCES TO DEFCON 3. INTELLI-
GENCE AND OPERATIONS REPORTS FROM SOUTH
KOREA AND CONFIRMATION FROM NATIONAL MEANS
INDICATE LARGE SCALE ARMED ATTACK AGAINST US
FORCES IN SOUTH KOREA AND RAPIDLY MOVING CON-

TINGENCY SITUATION. COMMANDERS WILL TAKE AP-
PROPRIATE ACTIONS TO ASSURE INCREASED READI-
NESS.

*By dawn of the second day, intelligence reports coming
in at a rate of almost 1,000 an hour were being received
simultaneously at the two military command centers and
the White House. They revealed that the situation in
Korea was getting much worse and Soviet military activities were increasing worldwide. Labeled "FLASH," a code
that takes priority over "ROUTINE" and "IMMEDIATE" messages, two of these reports had a special meaning to the
battle staff trying to untangle the stream of words and
symbols coming in by telephone, telex, and computer.
One report from the U.S. Air Force listening post at Ma-
rienfelde, in the suburbs of Berlin, reported Soviet aircraft
flying from their bases in the western U.S.S.R. to forward
sites in Eastern Europe. The other report, from U.S.S. Tal-
bot, a frigate on patrol in the North Atlantic, reported
harassment by Soviet aircraft.*

*As the pieces of the puzzle began to take shape for those
in the Pentagon trying to understand whether the Soviet
moves were part of a larger plan, more messages came in
from Korea. The 2nd Infantry Division reported troops
pouring over the border and exchanged fire with two bat-
talion-sized infantry units of North Korean regulars. The
U.S. division, estimating that a total of eight battalions of
North Koreans were across the border, had taken up defensive positions at Musan and the Imjin-gang River. The
fighting had begun, but the war was still a battle using
conventional weapons. It would not stay that way for
long, however; the feared nuclear "threshold" was about*

to be breached. A special top secret intelligence report from the commander in chief in Europe, headquartered at Vaihingen, outside Stuttgart, indicated how quickly the war might now spread.

FLASH
FROM: CINCEUR VAIHINGEN GE
TO: JCS WASHINGTON DC//J3 NMCC//
AIG 931
   TOP SECRET   U M B R A
   FG0284//OPREP-3 PINNACLE COMMAND ASSESS-
MENT//001//021950Z MAR 82//

   (TS/SI) ALL EVIDENCE IS THAT A MULTI-DIVISION OFFENSIVE AGAINST US AND NATO FORCES IN EUROPE IS BEING PREPARED. NO PRIOR STRATEGIC WARNING OTHER THAT EXERCISES OF COMMUNICATIONS SILENCE, SEMI-ANNUAL EXERCISE FOR MOBILIZATION CALL-UP OF RESERVISTS AND INCREASES IN MARITIME AIR PATROL ACTIVITY WAS OBSERVED. SIGINT AND RECONNAISSANCE REPORTS BARRACKS EVACUATION BY SOVIET AND EAST GERMAN FORCES. SOVIET FBM ACTIVITY IS REPORTED AT A HIGHER THAN NORMAL LEVEL IN THE NORTH ATLANTIC. RECOMMEND UPGRADE OF DEFENSE CONDITIONS AND DECISION ON RAPID REINFORCEMENT OF EUCOM FORCES FROM CONUS IAW REDCOM/EUCOM OPLAN 1760. ADDITIONAL REPORTS WILL FOLLOW.

The CINCEUR commander was reporting intelligence intercepts from his ground listening posts and also from his reconnaissance flights on the borders of East Germany and Czechoslovakia. He had decided to ask the generals in Washington to upgrade the readiness of all U.S. forces in Europe and to mobilize U.S. troop units in America that are committed to reinforce Europe in case of an invasion from the East. The Joint Chiefs agreed to upgrade the alert status to DEFCON-2, one short of "maximum readiness."

Toward the end of Day 2 the North Korean were pushing so quickly southward that the commander of the U.S. forces in Korea decided to evacuate a small arsenal of tactical nuclear artillery shells, W-48 155 mm and W-33 203 mm, from Camp Pelham, 4.8 miles from the DMZ. As a matter of course even the movement of nuclear weapons had to be recorded with the Pentagon.

At a few minutes past midnight on the third day, the stand-in president called a meeting of the National Security Council at the White House. Although the vice-president is theoretically in charge of crisis management, and would normally be operating from the White House Situation Room, the president decided to send him up in the "doomsday" plane, a converted Boeing 747 code named "Nightwatch." By ordering his vice-president aboard the plane, the president had made a major decision to disperse the so-called National Command Authorities, who include the president and the secretary of defense or their "duly deputized" alternates or successors. In effect, the president was creating a "reserve" commander in chief. The Nightwatch plane is fully equipped to run a nuclear war. It has a battle staff capable of duplicating the presidential codes for release of nuclear weapons and has all the plans and procedures required to oversee a nuclear exchange. It can stay aloft for more than 10 hours without refueling, and it can also be refueled by airborne tankers.

By dawn of the third day, key congressmen who actually took part in the exercise had been briefed on the quickly moving crisis, and defense readiness had been *raised to the maximum DEFCON-1: Cocked Pistol. An open communications link was prepared "internetting" the nuclear commanders with the president. Inside a command post in a granite mountain near Colorado Springs in the American Rockies, U.S. Air Force officers of the North American Aerospace Defense Command (NORAD) passed on the alert to their worldwide network of early-warning radar sites—Fylingdales in Yorkshire, Diyarbakir in eastern Turkey, Shemya and Clear in Alaska, Thule in Greenland, and the thirty-three sites of the aging bomber warning stations that stretch the entire width of the North American continent. All of these remote outposts buzzed with the frantic activity of the unfolding international emergency. The air defense warning was upgraded from "Yellow," a "probable" attack, to "Red." The code book describes "Red Alert" in sedate, unemotional terms: "An attack by hostile aircraft or missiles is imminent or is in progress." On computer consoles in the radar operations rooms, the alert code words flashed: Big Noise, Snow Man, Lemon Juice, and Apple Jack.*

Next, the secretary of defense decided it was time to evacuate "selected personnel" from Washington, D.C., by implementing the top secret Joint Emergency Evacuation Plan, or JEEP. Within thirty minutes, army and air force helicopters standing by at the Pentagon heliport and on the paved terrace between the Pentagon and the Potomac River had airlifted forty-four men and women—government officials, scientists, and technicians holding "JEEP-1" cards—to the Alternate National Military Command Center in Raven Rock and to the civilian government emergency bunker, known as the "Special Facility," in Mt. Weather in northern Virginia. JEEP cardholders are spe-

cially selected military and civilian functionaries who will help run the country during and after a nuclear war. They are on permanent standby and hold regular exercises to familiarize themselves with the procedure for getting to their dispersal points. Within four hours all JEEP cardholders had been flown to their assigned facilities— 59 went to the Special Facility at Mt. Weather, 194 to Raven Rock. The remaining four people from the Federal Emergency Management Agency (FEMA), the government civil defense agency, were taken to a secret location. Most probably it is the civil defense "National Warning Center" at Olney, Maryland.

Meanwhile, according to the incoming messages, the fighting in Korea worsened. American forces in Southwest Asia fought off Soviet air attacks. In Europe, NATO forces were attacked along a wide front and on the evening of 3 March word was received in Washington, D.C., that a U.S. ship on patrol in the North Atlantic Ocean had been sunk by a nuclear-armed AS-4 "Kitchen" cruise missile fired from a Soviet "Backfire" bomber. Two messages, arriving in quick succession, told the story. The first message, from the ship itself, bore the code word NUCFLASH, warning of an unidentified object on its missile radar. The second, coded FLASH NUDET (for nuclear detonation), was from the commander-in-chief of the Atlantic region (CIN-CLANT). Not only did it report the loss of a ship, it announced starkly the most important moment in the battle so far—the detonation of the first nuclear weapon of the war.

"This is a FLASH OVERRIDE OPREP-3 PINNACLE NUCFLASH report from the USS SPRUANCE as of 031920Z. At 031916Z, the USS SPRUANCE, at 6135N/0708E, detected what is be-

lieved to be a *Down Beat* radar signal from a visually unidentified object, but thought to be a nuclear armed air-launched cruise missile launched from a Backfire with the ship as an aim point. The object fell short by 700 meters and did not detonate. Ship is taking immediate evasive and defensive maneuvers. Amplifying information to follow."

The second message, of a second attack on the ship, read:

"This is reporting activity at echo victor charlie quebec romeo romeo, with an actual FLASH NUDET report, number zero zero one, field three: USS SPRUANCE, field four: 6135N, field five: 0708E, field six: zero three nineteen thirty four zulu, field seven: initial, field eight: air burst, Acknowledge. Out."

Up to this point the stand-in president had been reluctant to consider the use of nuclear weapons, or even to retaliate. At 0900 hours, however, an unexpected factor was thrown into his decision-making. A tank regiment successfully defending its position in the Fulda Gap in southern Germany, northeast of Frankfurt, reported a Soviet chemical attack resulting in a large number of casualties. The message arrived in Washington, D.C., in the following special format:

```
CIC: JGAA
FLASH
AIG 931
AIG 7806
CONFIDENTIAL
FD234/CHEMREP/001//
ABC/001/I//
PLATM/GE/FULDA/5033N/0948W/040851Z//
```

CASLTY/1200//
DEATHS/0745//
AMPN/ALL DIED WITHIN MINUTES, NO PROTECTIVE
MASKS USED//
DESCR/NERVE AGENT, PERSISTENT//
SYMPT/TIGHTNESS OF CHEST//
BASRPT/FROG MISSILE ATTACK/AGENT IDENTIFIED
BY DETECTION KIT//
AMPN/AGENT IDENTIFIED AS VICTOR XRAY//
RMKS/GROSS AREA DECONTAMINATION HALTED IN
ANTICIPATION OF FURTHER
ATTACKS/LARGE NUMBERS OF CIVILIAN CASUALTIES
EXPECTED. END.
DECL: 03 MAR 2000//

*The use of chemical weapons prompted an immediate
response from the stand-in president. From a number of
options provided to him by the Joint Chiefs, he chose a
"package" of nuclear weapons—nuclear artillery shells,
less than ten Lance missiles, and three nuclear bombs—
and ordered them to be used against Soviet forces in central Europe.*

*Throughout the day, as the tempo of the battle was
raised, the president also gave permission for regional
commanders elsewhere to use tactical nuclear weapons
"on a case-by-case basis." By mid-afternoon, the White
House had used the hot-line telex link to Moscow repeatedly to explain to the Kremlin the meaning of U.S. moves
in the hope of finding some way out of the mess. But the
situation only worsened. The Soviets destroyed U.S. satellites in an apparent attempt to disrupt military communications and early-warning surveillance.*

*Before the air force could replace the gaps in the U.S.
system by launching new satellites, the early-warning ra-*

dars of NORAD reported a massive Soviet missile attack on the United States. When the NORAD stations computed the trajectory and speed of the missiles, it became clear that the Soviet attack was aimed at "decapitating" the U.S. nuclear forces: The missiles would destroy command centers, the critical elements of government, and all means of worldwide communications. When the missiles hit, the White House was destroyed, the "president" was killed, and communications with the Pentagon went dead. Command of U.S. forces shifted immediately to the vice-president in the Nightwatch plane then circling somewhere over Ohio.

The only surviving means of communications left to the vice-president was the Minimum Essential Emergency Communications Network (MEECN), a collection of airborne command planes, very low frequency transmitters, and requisitioned commercial and research satellites. His first task was to locate the surviving forces and collect "damage assessment" reports. These reports would normally be compiled by the battle staff at Strategic Air Command headquarters near Omaha, Nebraska. Having established which of the forces had survived, the vice-president then used the "Airborne Launch Control System" aboard the Nightwatch plane to fire the remaining land-based missiles. Launching the bombers and the missiles on submarines presented more of a problem. To make contact with these forces, the vice-president had to use the special airborne communications planes belonging to Strategic Air Command (SAC) and the navy. They had all survived, were still airborne, and had reported in.

The vice-president, now the president, spoke with some of the surviving senior officers of SAC, NORAD, and the Joint

Chiefs of Staff to discuss courses of action. He had never before spoken to any of these men, the second tier of commanders, but he was already fully briefed on the four main options contained in the SIOP, and he saw only one real choice—to implement the retaliatory strike, known as the "Major Attack Option." By the end of the fifth day, thousands of U.S. nuclear warheads were on their way to hit targets in the Soviet Union.

At the government's civil defense bunkers in Maynard, Massachusetts, and Denton, Texas, a cadre of government officials who had flown there on the third day was still alive. They began the enormous task of trying to reconstitute a nation.

*   *   *

Ivy League was an extremely elaborate, expensive, and unusual war game. Unlike other major war games, it was not designed to test whether airplanes could fly, ships could sail, or missiles and guns could fire—or whether Warsaw Pact tanks could overwhelm NATO forces in Europe or Soviet-backed divisions in North Korea could successfully invade the South. It was not even designed to test the Pentagon's version of "crisis management"—the basic steps of how to get out of a sticky political tussle with the Russians without slipping into a full-scale nuclear war. In Ivy League, the Pentagon planners assumed that these things would go horribly wrong for the Western Alliance, that the Soviet Union would be successful in all its military adventures, and that the two superpowers would indulge in "escalatory exchanges of thermonuclear weapons . . . culminating in a major strategic nuclear exchange" between the two of them. Millions would be left dead on both sides.

Ivy League, however, was not concerned with casualties. The central purpose of the war game, according to
the Defense Department brief, was to "exercise and evaluate plans and procedures associated with the Single Integrated Operational Plan (SIOP)." For the first time since
the mid-1950s, the generals had set themselves the problem of surviving a missile attack and of functioning with
impaired communications as a fighting unit in a devastated environment. Their primary task was to make sure
that the command structure survived. The key civilian
actors in Ivy League—former Secretary of State William
Rogers played the president and ex-CIA director Richard
Helms played the vice-president—had to be protected if
the established civilian control over the use of nuclear
weapons was to be maintained. Their command posts and
their communications had to have an "enduring" quality;
otherwise, there would be no means of executing the
SIOP. As one official who took part in Ivy League remarked, "Protection of key government functions during
a crisis is as much of a deterrent to nuclear war as building
new strategic nuclear systems." When it was all over and
"President Rogers" was buried deep in the rubble of the
White House, President Reagan selflessly suggested the
war game "ultimately help[ed] us prove that our adversaries have nothing to gain by such an attack."

The underlying reason for Ivy League was that the U.S.
government now believes that the American nuclear deterrent is no longer credible unless the United States can
demonstrate that its commanders, their command posts,
and their communications links can withstand a nuclear
attack and fight a prolonged nuclear war. Nuclear weapons have become so finely tuned and so accurate that the

leaders of the two superpowers can now make selective nuclear strikes against each other for months on end—as long as the commanders survive. That is the theory on which the new strategic doctrine is based.

It is all a far cry from the 1950s' doctrine of "massive retaliation" or the Johnson days of "mutual assured destruction" or the Nixon days of "controlled responses." Today, nuclear planners have designed something more "rational" than these single massive blows, or "spasm responses," as they used to call them. War planning is no longer a question of selecting a handful of military targets —the Kremlin and Communist party headquarters, some industrial plants, a few railways and bridges—and blowing them up all at once. War planning is now an extremely complicated and technically sophisticated art. There are more than 40,000 potential targets, and the SIOP contains numerous options and sub-options for major and minor strikes. The arsenal contains more than 10,000 deliverable strategic nuclear weapons ranging in size from about fifty kilotons (four times the size of the Hiroshima bomb) to nine megatons (seven hundred times the size of the Hiroshima bomb). The missiles' accuracies range from 600 feet to almost a mile. The megatonnage, accuracy, and number of missiles in conjunction with the number and type of the targets allow the planners to formulate many choices for any commander who survives the first attack long enough to keep his finger on the button.

By playing Ivy League, the generals demonstrated the vulnerability of at least part of their command structure: The president was dead and the National Military Command Center in the Pentagon was out of action. The vice-president had lived but his only surviving means of communications was a relatively precarious one—from a flying bunker. The only way of "ensuring" the deterrent, said the generals, was to spend a lot more money on something they call C^3I.

Pronounced C-cubed-I, this cryptic formula covers any of the Pentagon's activities that deal with commanding, controlling, and communicating with its forces. It also covers the collection of military intelligence, the "I" of the formula. The entire C^3I program costs the Pentagon $30 billion a year to run, a sum that includes everything from the missile early-warning stations to the computers supplying allied information to NATO to the smallest military telephone exchange at the most distant outpost of American military reach. By far the largest single part of C^3I falls under the category "strategic"—those systems covering the use of nuclear weapons. Strategic C^3I costs about $8 billion a year to operate and it acts as the nervous system of the nuclear arsenal, in other words, the head of the scorpion, or the software that runs the hardware.

C^3I has had little popular attention because it is somewhat difficult to focus on. It is not a single war machine, like a missile, an airplane, or a submarine; it is a vast, heterogeneous system of early-warning satellites, radars, and computers, communications relays, and underground and airborne control rooms. The system is used to execute and to create the SIOP. Military intelligence tells war planners what targets should be selected and shows them where they are and what would happen to the Soviet war machine if they were destroyed.

Recently, the Pentagon planners have declared that the C^3I system is in such poor shape that it cannot perform its two key nuclear functions adequately. It cannot be counted on to provide enough information to the right people during a surprise nuclear attack for the "right" decision to be made, and it cannot provide the communications and control system that would allow the president, or his successor, to stay in touch with the strategic forces during nuclear war. Ivy League, they say, proved them right.

But why have the generals suddenly "discovered" the C^3I problem? It has been there ever since the Russians made their first successful test of an intercontinental missile. The fact is the generals never gave the C^3I problem their full attention; it was always more satisfying to the military ego to be ordering up a new generation of missiles, bombers, or submarines than it was to be concerned about new generations of computers. Few generals bothered to learn about communications; this knowledge would not have aided their career prospects. But Jimmy Carter changed all that.

Of all the presidents since Harry Truman, Carter took the greatest interest in the contingency plans for nuclear war. Within weeks of arriving at the White House in January 1977, Carter, a former member of a submarine crew, ordered a full review of the presidential procedures for the release of nuclear weapons. He was especially interested in the civilian chain of command should the president become incapacitated. Carter was astounded to find that the next commander in line, the vice-president, had never been involved, in any administration, in any of the top secret briefings about the SIOP and its attack options so he ordered a series of secret briefings for himself, his vice-president, Walter Mondale, and his secretary of defense, Harold Brown. Carter's preoccupation with the

SIOP percolated down through his administration and within a year a review of the whole nuclear response procedures was well under way. The result was a series of presidential directives, the most famous of which was No. 59, which appeared in the summer of 1980.

PD-59, as it is known, was the first executive order requiring the armed forces of the United States to be able to fight a prolonged nuclear war. According to Carter, the nation needed a C^3I system that could "endure" such a war: Endurance had replaced assured destruction as a minimum essential requirement for U.S. strategic forces. To the generals this meant that computers, satellites, radars, and communication links suddenly had equal priority with missiles, airplanes, and submarines. It also meant war games like Ivy League. To the members of the new Reagan administration, who willingly inherited PD-59, it meant an opportunity for some tough talk about fighting nuclear wars and actually winning them. President Reagan said it was possible to "win" a nuclear war; so did Vice-President Bush. Asked how this could happen Bush replied, "You have a survivability of command and control, survivability of industrial potential, protection of a percentage of your citizens, and you have a capability that inflicts more damage on the opposition that it can inflict upon you. That's the way you have a winner."

Given the early belligerence of the Reagan administration, many people harbored the not unreasonable suspicion that, if the administration thought a nuclear war was winnable, they might try it. But, on closer examination, it has emerged that Reagan's nuclear war policy is based on PD-59; the fighting of a nuclear war was initially a Carter, not a Reagan, doctrine. The question was rightly asked:

Had President Carter radically altered the contingency plans to respond to a nuclear attack? Was PD-59 a revolutionary step? Or was it, as Carter's defense secretary, Harold Brown, claimed, just an evolutionary growth in the nuclear war plans that had been in existence since Hiroshima and Nagasaki?

The gap between presidential rhetoric and actual war plans, between the government's posturing and what would actually happen if the SIOP were implemented, has existed from the beginning of the nuclear age. When Truman's hot-headed secretary of state, James Byrnes, attended the postwar peace conferences with the Russians he always arrived in a cocky mood because of America's nuclear monopoly. He used to swagger into the meetings as if he were carrying an atomic bomb in his hip pocket, according to the secretary of war at that time, Henry Stimson. In those days, when the American arsenal of nuclear bombs could be counted on the fingers of one hand, the gap between rhetoric and reality was of small consequence. As the stockpile of nuclear weapons has grown in size and sophistication, the size and nature of the gap have become the central question, and yet this question has also become increasing difficult to answer. The question can only be properly addressed by going back to the beginning.

2

Incipient Power

NO self-respecting bomber pilot, who flew in the romanticized age of propeller-driven warplanes and dropped the conventional bombs of World War II, would join a squadron whose crest and motto hinted at anything less than total destruction. "Strike Hard, Strike Sure" demanded the motto of the RAF's Bomber Command, and the crests of its squadrons carried images signifying power, cunning, supremacy, and death. America's flying units were born with similar crests and mottoes, with one important exception: Strategic Air Command. The nuclear age and the emerging policy of deterrence through assured destruction demanded something less belligerent, something that would reflect America's new dual role as peacekeeper and protector. Bomber pilots needed a new image, something to take the public mind off the horror of Hiroshima and Nagasaki, something that would rationalize the bomber's continued role in society. For SAC's new emblem the generals chose a mailed fist on a background of blue sky with fluffy white clouds, and in

the fist they put three red lightning bolts *plus* a prominent green olive branch. For a motto they chose Peace Is
Our Profession—surely one of the finest examples of the
advertising copywriter's art ever to come out of the
United States. Madison Avenue could not have done better.

The emblem first went on public display inside the
gates of SAC headquarters at Offutt Air Force Base near
Omaha, Nebraska, in 1952, the sixth anniversary of the
elite air force command that had been formed after the
war as America's nuclear strike force. In charge was the
bomber veteran of World War II, General Curtis E.
LeMay, who had personally chosen the emblem from
more than 60 entries submitted by members of the SAC.

The new emblem and its motto were certainly an accurate portrayal of the postwar dilemma in which the
United States found itself: striving toward peace and
progress on the one hand, and toward war preparedness
on the other. But the new emblem also masked the true
nature of what was going on at Offutt Air Force Base,
where the profession was hardly pursuing peace.

In the four years he had been at SAC, LeMay had transformed a loosely knit, somewhat neglected unit of the
postwar air force with all its problems of demobilization,
overseas occupation, and budget restrictions into the
dominant force in America's operational planning for nuclear war. The air force had created a mobile command
capable of fulfilling America's highest priority mission: an
atomic offensive, as LeMay put it, "in one fell swoop,
telescoping mass and time" against the Soviet Union. He
had increased the number of bombers capable of carrying
atomic weapons from 60 to almost 300. His bomber crews

were highly trained, with special navigational aids that LeMay had encouraged them to develop. Each time they flew they carried detailed maps of their assigned Soviet targets showing all known geographical features. In the late 1940s, when there were only a few atomic bombs in the U.S. arsenal, those targets were the largest Soviet urban-industrial centers, a handful of the largest airfields, and the largest ports. By the mid-1950s between 5,000 and 6,000 targets, from big cities to small industries and tiny river crossings, had been identified by U.S. intelligence: SAC forces had plans to hit 1,700 of them, 409 of which were airfields. Since this could not be done all at once, LeMay was working toward an "optimum plan" that called for an initial strike of about 700 bombs dropped by aircraft approaching the Soviet Union from several directions at the same time. The whole operation would take about two hours from the moment the bombers crossed the Soviet early-warning radar screen to the end of the mission, the planes using a "bomb-as-you-go" system of attack. Any bombs left over would be dropped on Moscow.

High-ranking officers visiting SAC headquarters were given an outline briefing of the plan with maps of the Soviet Union penetrated by heavy black lines progressively converging on Moscow. Each target was pinpointed with multicolored stars. "The final impression," wrote a naval officer, Captain William Moore, "was that virtually all of Russia would be nothing but a smoking, radiating ruin at the end of two hours." No one, not even the president or the Joint Chiefs of Staff, cared to know the exact manner in which such an attack would be carried out: The details were left to General LeMay and his staff.

In those days of America's atomic monopoly, if President Truman had ever decided to "press the button" because the Soviet Union threatened the future of the free world, LeMay would decide what to do with his forces, how to fight the war, and, most important, how to win it. In theory, the war would not start with a preemptive strike. U.S. national policy is that atomic weapons should be used only in a defensive action, but LeMay was careful not to rule out a preemptive action because he wanted to cover all contingencies. Asked at the time whether his war plans squared with national policy, LeMay replied, "I have heard this thought [no preemption] stated many times and it sounds very fine. However, it is not in keeping with United States history. Just look and note who started the Revolutionary War, the War of 1812, the Indian Wars, and the Spanish-American Wars. I want to make it clear that I am not advocating a preventive war; however, I believe that if the U.S. is pushed in the corner far enough we would not hesitate to strike first."

In fact, LeMay had never had any thought of creating a force with a retaliatory capability; it was always the first punch that mattered. The last war had ended with the United States having the capability to inflict total destruction and that, as far as LeMay was concerned, was how the next one would begin. Such thoughts prompted almost no dissent in the immediate postwar period: Strategic bombing was an accepted doctrine at the Pentagon, which is the reason the spearhead of the postwar air force was named Strategic Air Command.

The doctrine of bombing civilians as a way of winning wars—the theory being that the ones who survived would not want to fight—had a short history. It started with

Mussolini's air offensive on Ethiopia in 1935 and continued with Japan's sorties on Chinese cities in 1937 and the German attack on the Spanish town of Guernica. During World War II both the Luftwaffe and the Allied air forces found they could not bomb military or industrial targets accurately so they settled for the terror bombing of civilans and called it "strategic" bombing. The Allies hit Berlin, then Dresden, and then fire-bombed Tokyo. The climax of the new military philosophy was Hiroshima and Nagasaki. Although there was no evidence to say strategic bombing worked—in fact there was plenty of evidence to say civilian populations were not cowed by it—the American air commanders carried this policy of holy war into the postwar era, declaring, as LeMay did, that the purpose of the postwar world was "to make the existence of civilization subject to the good will and the good sense of men who control the employment of air power."

LeMay produced an annual contingency war plan suggesting ways in which the small arsenal of nuclear weapons might be used. In theory, this plan was drawn up according to guidance from the Joint Chiefs of Staff (JCS). The guidance, suggesting what targets should be hit and what level of damage should be inflicted—light, moderate, or severe—was contained in Annex C of the JCS global contingency plan known as the Joint Strategic Capabilities Plan. The key word was "capabilities." With only a handful of nuclear weapons available, fewer than 50 up to 1949, it was obvious that the war plan would use them all; the only question was how. SAC was supposed to submit the plans directly to the JCS for review and approval, although LeMay became so independent that from 1951 until 1955 the JCS never received a copy of the plans:

LeMay considered the details of operational planning a closely guarded secret and simply refused to let anyone know what they were. He could have been ordered to produce them, of course, and eventually he was, but for six crucial years America's nuclear war planning was unregulated.

LeMay got away with it largely because of the lack of involvement of the executive branch. In the immediate postwar years, President Truman was solely concerned with obtaining some kind of international control over atomic weapons; he believed they could be outlawed, like poison gases had been in 1925. Moreover, he thought he had enough control of America's nuclear arsenal because he had established two rules: Only the president was allowed to make the decision to use the weapons, and only the president could approve any increases in the production of fissionable material and, therefore, of new weapons. In reality, however, Truman abdicated his control. He established a three-man committee composed of the secretaries of state and defense and the chairman of the Atomic Energy Commission to advise him on all aspects of nuclear policy; Truman "decided" what to do only after a clear consensus had emerged from this triumvirate, thus effectively delegating one of the major areas of presidential power to these men. The powerful Joint Committee on Atomic Energy also contributed toward the erosion of executive control. Established by the 1946 McMahon Act that brought the production of nuclear materials under civilian control, the committee was led by Senator Brien McMahon, a nuclear weapons zealot, who believed the American arsenal of atomic bombs could not be too large. McMahon liked to be known as "Mr. Atom," and he once told the Senate that he thought the bombing of Hiroshima had been "the greatest event in world history since the birth of Jesus Christ." His committee's influence would become so extensive in pushing for increases in the nuclear weapons production line that it blurred the traditional division between the executive and legislative branches whereby the executive decides policy with the final consent of Congress. In atomic matters the Congress would decide policy with the advice and consent of the executive.

The overall lack of presidential direction and control created a policy vacuum that allowed several interacting factors to push America, willy-nilly, into building a bigger and bigger arsenal of nuclear weapons. As intelligence-gathering techniques in the Soviet Union improved, more targets were identified. At SAC headquarters, LeMay was always ready to revise his bomb requirements upward in order to hit the new targets intelligence had discovered, and the White House and Congress could always be persuaded to step up production of nuclear weapons to fill LeMay's orderbook. At the same time, the scientists and engineers at the atomic weapons laboratories were refining the production of the bombs to make them more powerful, yet smaller and lighter, so that they could be carried to their targets not just by large bombers, but also by medium and small bombers and eventually by rockets and missiles. All of these factors—improved intelligence rooting out new targets, disinterest at the White House, the failure of Congressional regulation, and the steady technological advances in the bomb business—were central to the evolution of a series of SAC war plans. Code named Halfmoon, Broiler, Frolic, Grabber, Fleetwood,

Doublestar, Trojan, Offtackle, Shakedown, and Cross-piece, each plan was more comprehensive than the last, each leading the United States swiftly down the path to the age of massive retaliation, overkill, and war fighting. In those early days, the war plans were put together with little thought given to overall objectives, such as, How many bombs would be needed to ensure victory? What would the effect of hundreds of bombs exploding on Soviet soil have on the "conquered" Russian population or on world opinion? Would a massive nuclear attack eliminate communism forever? Would America be seen as a savior or a butcher? Generals like LeMay had no time for such questions. In military jargon these war plans were known as "capabilities" plans: You made use of everything you had. In his memoirs, LeMay would put it like this, "Our job in SAC was not to promulgate a national policy or an international one. Our job was to produce. And we produced. We put America in that situation of incipient power which she occupied at the time." LeMay never discussed with the president or even the air force chief of staff "what we were going to do with the force we had or what we should do with it, or anything of that sort." The rule of thumb was, if it's in the stockpile, use it, and if it's not there, get it.

In retrospect, the lack of presidential knowledge about, or control over, nuclear war planning at the operational level is stunning. The executive branch had no clear idea of where America's nuclear policy, or lack of it, was leading. An American historian, David Rosenberg, who has done some of the most insightful work on the early nuclear war plans, points out, "What Truman and the National Security Council apparently did not foresee was that increasing numbers of prospective Soviet targets, the growing complexity of atomic weapons and their delivery systems, improvements in Soviet air defenses and Soviet acquisition of atomic bombs would require increasingly rigid operational planning, a trend which would steadily reduce the choices available to the president in a nuclear confrontation." Indeed, those "choices" of how to use the nuclear arsenal were already blurred and the question of whether SAC would actually have been used for a preemptive strike still remains open. "Although it was generally understood that the United States would not act as the aggressor or attempt to provoke war, no high national policy decision in the gray area of preemption was ever made," says Rosenberg.

In early 1948 the National Security Council began to discuss a policy statement on nuclear war. It emerged as National Security Council Document No. 30 (NSC 30), and it did two things. First, the policy mandated that, in the event of hostilities, the National Military Establishment—the new term for the American military machine—"must be ready to utilize promptly and effectively all appropriate means available, including atomic weapons, in the interest of national security and must plan accordingly." Second, NSC 30 placed the ultimate decision "as to the employment of atomic weapons in the event of war" in the hands of the president. However, it said nothing about when and how such weapons should be used or what sorts of targets should be hit first. Was the purpose of a war to destroy the Soviet people, its industry, the Communist party, the Communist hierarchy, or a combination of these? Should there be a requirement to occupy, possibly reconstruct, Russia after victory or should the country be "sealed off," letting it work out its own salvation, as one air force general put it? Because of the intense secrecy about all atomic matters and the increasing number of classification categories, it was almost impossible for members of the National Security Council to hold a productive discussion about atomic policy. They had one overriding principle, however: Any public debate of the possibility of *not* using atomic weapons was unacceptable. It could encourage the Russians into thinking America might hesitate to use its atomic weapons, and it could discourage the trust put in Washington by America's European allies. Two paragraphs of NSC 30 are chillingly explicit on this.

Paragraph No. 5 reads: "In this matter, public opinion must be recognized as a factor of considerable importance. Deliberation or decision on a subject of this significance, even if clearly affirmative, might have the effect of placing before the American people a moral question of vital security significance at a time when the full security impact of the question had not become apparent. If this decision is to be made by the American people, it should be made in the circumstances of an actual emergency when the principal factors involved are in the forefront of public consideration." In other words, the American public in a state of war fever would be likely to accept the use of nuclear weapons.

Paragraph No. 7 speaks for itself: "Were the United States to decide *against* [emphasis added] or publicly debate the issue of the use of the atomic bomb on moral grounds, this country might gain the praise of the world's radical fringe and would certainly receive the applause of the Soviet bloc, but the United States would be thoroughly condemned by every sound citizen in Western Europe, whose enfeebled security this country would obviously be threatening."

The Pentagon's guidance to LeMay was fairly general: The Joint Chiefs picked out targets they thought ought to be in the war plan and told LeMay what sort of damage should be done to them. The rest was up to LeMay, and he had plenty of time. A 1948 Pentagon study assumed that war would not occur between the two emerging superpowers until Russia had between 100 and 200, or more, atomic weapons. That would not be until 1964 according to intelligence estimates of the day. In fact, these estimates were hopelessly out of line: The Soviet Union was only months away from exploding its first nuclear device and, by 1952, according to the JCS, already had 50 deliverable atomic weapons.

U.S. intelligence of Soviet activities in those early postwar years was erratic and often simply wrong. Estimates in Washington might have been better if Truman had allowed more people to share their information about his "sacred trust," as he called the atomic bomb. As it was, only the triumvirate of two cabinet officers and the chairman of the Atomic Energy Commission plus a handful of military officers, perhaps literally ten or so people, knew the exact atomic capability of the United States—how many bombs the U.S. had and how many they could produce in an emergency. On the specific question of when the Soviet Union would produce its first weapon, Truman mistakenly took the word of Leslie Groves, the general who had run the Manhattan Project. Groves was an engineer and an excellent manager who had successfully

completed America's bomb project under arduous wartime conditions, but he had little experience of, nor much
aptitude for, international political analysis. He considered the Russians so backward and battered by the war
that they would have great difficulty building an atomic
bomb. He also believed that because the United States
and Britain had bought up most of the then-known uranium deposits in the then Belgian Congo the Russian
bomb-builders would not be able to find enough of their
own. Any geologist could have told Groves that that was
most unlikely; the Soviet Union had such a vast landmass
there was bound to be some uranium somewhere and, in
any case, the Russians now had access to plentiful uranium mines in Czechoslovakia. Ignoring this, Groves told
Truman it would take the Russians twenty years to build
a bomb, and, as such, he contributed to the president's
remoteness in overseeing the growth of the atomic arsenal and the plans for nuclear war.

No such remoteness existed at Offutt Air Force Base,
where LeMay's boys were being molded into America's
elite fighting force. "It took some time to get the Air
Force educated on what an atomic bomb was," said
LeMay, but "after this permeated down far enough and
enough people knew we were really in a position to take
some action, [the bomb] began to take hold." LeMay's
task was twofold: crew training and war planning. There
was no war plan in 1948. "This didn't worry me very much
because they [the U.S. Air Force] didn't have any capability for war anyway," said LeMay. "They may have had
something in the file about go and take the high ground
around Gettysburg or something of that general nature,
but a war plan as I understood it, what targets you were

going to destroy, and what the timing was going to be, and where you were going to do it from and what outfit was going to do it, and all the details, no, they didn't have anything like that."

As the plans took shape, LeMay was reluctant to let anyone know what they were, and even the SAC briefing for privileged officers from the Pentagon would not give much away. Typically the briefing would start with a historical review of the U.S. Air Force's strategic bombing record during World War II. The review would show the appalling losses over Germany and compare them with the swifter, and more decisive, air battle over Japan that ended with the use of the atomic bomb. During 49 months of operations against Germany, the U.S. lost 10,000 bombers (the RAF lost 12,000), whereas they lost only 485 in a 14-month war with Japan. Great emphasis was put on the high standard of training of the aircrews—even to the point of undergoing a rigorous survival course to show how they would perform if they were shot down over enemy territory. Each crew would be sent to a remote desert region of Nevada and turned loose with "nothing but a few fish hooks and a pocket knife." The men had to make their own way back to "free territory" while evading SAC "enemy forces." This "separated the men from the boys," as one SAC officer put it.

On arrival at SAC, LeMay had been shocked to find that "no one was really proficient at their trade," and LeMay's answer was the time-honored military training code of humiliation followed by rewards for improvement. To show the SAC aircrews how bad they were, LeMay organized an operational mission against Dayton, Ohio. "I ran the whole command at it and not one crew finished the mission as briefed," LeMay recalled; "once everyone agreed they had a job to do then we settled down and did some work." LeMay instituted a grading system for the aircrews. The best were the "Select" crews, the second best were known as "Lead" crews. Any Select crew member was eligible for "spot" promotion for excellence in his work, but if, for some reason, the Select crew lost its special rating, all members of the crew with "spot" promotion would automatically revert to their previous rank. Each of the Select and Lead crews was given a target folder containing the available data on one Soviet target and they spent their time studying all possible methods of attack. While the citizens of the United States slept peacefully in their beds, SAC aircrews made simulated bombing runs on industrial areas across the country using radar bomb scoring units on the ground, which would track the bombers as they came toward the target and give them a score over the target according to when the bombardier released the bomb. The training was relentless. The war planners, like LeMay, believed they held the future of civilization in their hands and the more they felt the supreme importance of their role, the more they were afraid it might be taken away from them. Sooner or later, they knew, the navy would begin to play a part in the nuclear business. The navy had planes that could drop nuclear bombs just as well as the air force; they also had submarines and eventually would use them to dispatch nuclear warheads attached to submarine-launched missiles. The navy had to be kept at bay. An air force staff officer warned in 1948, "If the Greyhound Bus Company can demonstrate a capability of delivering [atomic] bombs better than any other agency, that company will get the job."

Soviet targets were coded according to type—a city, a factory, a port, or an airfield—and to their relevance to the war-making capacity of the Soviet Union and then listed in the annually prepared Emergency War Plan. The targets were given special codes: Bravo, for targets that "blunted" the Soviet capability to deliver an atomic offensive, mostly airfields; Delta, for targets that "disrupted" the vital elements of the Soviet war-making capacity; and, after the signing of the North Atlantic Treaty in 1949, they added Romeo, for any target that "retarded" Soviet advances into Western Europe. Until 1950 the Delta mission, basically targets of the Soviet urban-industrial base, was given priority, but following the explosion of the Russians' first atomic bomb, the Bravo mission surged ahead to the number one priority on LeMay's target list.

LeMay's bombs were to be delivered by the B-36 and the B-47. The first B-52 squadron was not operational until 1956. The B-36 had a range of 8,000 miles at 40,000 feet, or 8,800 miles at 30,000 feet. The medium B-47 had a range of 5,600 miles using one in-flight refueling, or 7,800 miles using two refuelings. In 1949 the prototype B-50, christened "Lucky Lady Two," made the first nonstop, air-refueled, aerial circumnavigation of the globe. The 23,452-mile flight took 94 hours. When it was over, LeMay observed that the United States could "deliver an atom bomb to any spot on earth where it may be required." The bombs they carried had changed little from the Mark 3 "Fat Man" plutonium bomb dropped on Nagasaki, but they were becoming progressively lighter and more powerful. The Mark 4 was in the arsenal in 1948–49 and the Mark 6, the first nuclear weapon to be mass produced, entered the U.S. stockpile in 1951. It weighed 8,500 pounds (almost 2,000 pounds lighter than Fat Man) and was 128 inches long and 61 inches in diameter.

Soon LeMay was no less confident about the ability of his bombardiers to hit their targets. The SAC standard visitor's briefing contained some astonishingly optimistic predictions about bombing accuracy—something that had been notoriously bad during World War II. In 1941, for example, the RAF bombardiers found it difficult to drop their bombs within a radius of five miles of the target, and in 1946, during the first testing of an atomic bomb, in the Pacific Ocean, the bomb missed its orange-painted stationary battleship "target" by more than half a mile. But in the early 1950s SAC boasted that they could place 50 percent of all their bombs within a radius of about 1,400 feet of the target with radar, or blind, bombing and within 600 feet if they could actually see the target. The "Select" crews were said to do even better. LeMay was also confident that his bombers would be able to penetrate Soviet air defenses. SAC's simulated attacks on the United States had shown that it was extremely difficult to prevent penetration of coordinated heavy bomber attacks that hit the early warning radar screen from many directions simultaneously. SAC's use of electronic countermeasures, such as "chaff," or strips of metal dropped from the bomber, was shown to be effective against radar for the new Soviet guided missiles because the radar could not distinguish between the bombers and the "chaff."

By 1952, LeMay considered that he could win a war

with the Soviet Union in thirty days compared with an estimated sixty days when he had taken over SAC. There was never any doubt in LeMay's mind that he would have access to the civilian-controlled nuclear stockpile "when the bell rings" and no question that the atomic bombs would be used. Asked by a visiting naval officer, "Is SAC prepared to conduct strategic air warfare in case the use of atomic weapons is outlawed?" LeMay replied, "You sailor boys are always asking this foolish question. It is inconceivable to me that this situation will ever arise."

Operating on the long leash allowed him by the White House and the Joint Chiefs, LeMay always had two troubling questions: How fast could the bombs be built to satisfy his demand and how fast could he get enough planes to carry them? In 1948, there were fewer than fifty bombs in the arsenal and none of these was assembled. They were all Mark 3, plutonium bombs like the one dropped at Nagasaki and took thirty-nine men more than two days to put each one together. The bombs were so large and heavy—each weighed 10,000 pounds—that they could only be loaded on their bombers with the aid of a hoist in a specially built, eight-foot-deep pit under the aircraft's bomb bay.

The first SAC Emergency War Plans always called for more atomic bombs than the planes could possibly deliver. Through 1948 SAC had only thirty B-29s modified to drop the Mark 3, yet the December 1948 war plan, code named Trojan, called for attacks on seventy cities with 133 atomic bombs. Bomb production had to be increased substantially to meet the target of 400 bombs that the air force commanders had originally asked for following the successful atomic tests in the Pacific in 1947.

The man who had to evaluate these requests was the civilian custodian of the nuclear stockpile, the chairman of the Atomic Energy Commission, David Lilienthal. When he took over the commission in 1947, he had been shocked to find that the nuclear cupboard was virtually bare, but now he was horrified at the rate at which the air force was demanding more. The generals were beginning to order atomic weapons "like mess kits and rifles," as he noted at the time, and he decided that it was time for President Truman to curb the generals' hunger for more bombs. Lilienthal had every reason to believe that he would receive a sympathetic hearing from the president. At Lilienthal's urging, Truman had already rejected a united Pentagon offensive to acquire custody of the nuclear weapons materials from the AEC. But before Lilienthal had a chance to make his case, the Russians exploded their first atomic bomb and, in the new climate of fear, Truman decided it was no time to stall expansion. The momentous decision to go ahead with the production of the H-bomb followed in January 1950. The age of overkill was born.

A short, stark summary of the SAC Emergency War Plan approved by the Joint Chiefs on 22 October 1951 appears in Volume IV (1950–1952) of *The History of the Joint Chiefs of Staff*. It was the only plan actually approved by the JCS between 1951 and 1955. The summary says, "The initial strike would be launched on approximately $D+6$ days [the sixth day after the start of hostilities]. Heavy bombers flying from Maine would drop 20 bombs in the Moscow-Gorky area and return to the United Kingdom. Simultaneously, medium bombers from Labrador would attack the Leningrad area with 12 weapons and reassemble at British bases. Meanwhile, medium bombers based in the British Isles would approach the U.S.S.R. along the edge of the Mediterranean Sea and deliver 52 bombs in the industrial regions of the Volga and Donets Basin; they would return through Libyan and Egyptian airfields. More medium bombers flying from the Azores would drop 15 weapons in the Caucasus area and then stage through Dhahran, Saudi Arabia. Concurrently, medium bombers from Guam would bring 15 bombs against Vladivostock and Irkutsk." In the Pentagon, two important warnings were sounded about the demanding war plans and the burgeoning arsenals, but neither would ultimately slow down the rate of accumulation of atomic weapons. One voice came from the navy and another from an ad hoc committee composed of senior army, navy, and air force officers set up to review the strategic implications of an air war with the Soviet Union. Warnings by both groups showed that, while the expansion of the nuclear stockpile certainly filled the demands of the SAC operational planners, it did not solve the problems of the strategic planners: If the aim was to bring about capitulation, destroy the roots of communism, or critically weaken the power of the Soviet leadership to dominate their people, the use of nuclear weapons wasn't going to work. Nor would atomic blasts "liberate" the Soviet people from the tyranny of Stalin. In the end, atomic weapons were too powerful; there would be nothing left to set free.

The navy had little influence on the burgeoning nuclear arsenal because its submarines were not yet operational and, therefore, the admirals could view what was going on at SAC headquarters more objectively, if somewhat jealously. One of them, Rear Admiral Daniel Gallery, the assistant chief of naval operations for guided missiles, wrote a memo questioning the effects of implementing SAC's 1949 strike plan. Admiral Gallery asserted that it was wrong for a civilized society like the United States to have as its broad purpose in war "simply [the] destruction and annihilation of the enemy," adding the memorable line, "leveling large cities has a tendency to alienate the affections of the inhabitants and does not create an atmosphere of goodwill after the war."

Gallery's memo was the first Pentagon document to advocate a "no cities" war plan. The second document, from an interservice ad hoc committee led by U.S. Air Force Lieutenant-General H. R. Harmon, was also critical of the net effects of bombing cities, albeit from a different standpoint. Even if all of the 133 bombs called for in the Trojan war plan were to land and explode on target, concluded Harmon, they would only achieve a 30–40 percent reduction in industrial capacity and the Russians would still have sufficient troop mobility to be able to invade "selected areas" of Western Europe, the Middle East, and the Far East. Nevertheless, the committee emphasized that a nuclear weapon was "the only means of inflicting shock and serious damage to vital elements of the Soviet war-making capacity [and] the advantages of its early use would be transcending." Although he had criticized the military's faith in the destructive power of the early atomic war plans, Harmon had also endorsed them and had urged an increase in production of the bombs.

The Harmon report, plus the Soviet explosion of an atomic bomb, led to an important re-think about Russian targets. The problem had always been the vastness of the enemy's territory and the lack of good military intelligence. Before the U-2 and satellite reconnaissance, the target maps used by the SAC pilots were often based on pre–World War II surveys and, at best, SAC aerial photographs of Germany taken between 1942 and 1943. The selection of targets was, to put it kindly, haphazard. The air force operational planners had to think in terms of what they could find to hit, not what some strategist in the Pentagon thought they should hit. The airmen talked rather loosely about the "bonus effect" of hitting cities with major industrial plants, but their primary aim up to 1949 was the destruction of heavily populated areas. It just happened that because most Soviet workers live close to their workplaces these were also, for the most part, industrial areas. War plan Broiler in 1947 called for 34 bombs to be dropped on 24 cities; war plan Trojan, one year later, targeted 70 cities with 133 bombs; and war plan Offtackle, in 1949, called for 220 bombs on 104 cities, with 72 weapons in reserve.

After the explosion of the Russian bomb, the JCS began to add airfields as priority targets in the hope of preventing the Soviet Air Force from launching an atomic attack on the United States. The JCS also added a new industrial category, "atomic energy industries," to the list of priority targets in the hope of retarding the Soviet bomb project. Identifying these targets became a matter of high priority. To make an atomic bomb you need uranium and huge amounts of electricity and, in those days, huge factories. As the Americans had done, the Russians were using the gaseous diffusion technique to separate the fissionable U-235 from its more abundant cousin, U-238. The American gaseous diffusion separation plant at Oak Ridge,

Tennessee, where the U-235 for the first American bomb had been produced, was four stories high and each side of its U-shaped structure was half a mile long. When running at full capacity, it used as much electricity as the city of New York.

The main problem was still pinpointing the location of these specialized targets. SAC's approach was unsophisticated, to say the least. The air force didn't know where all the Soviet power plants were, nor had they calculated how much damage could be expected to the plants from an attack nor had they estimated the minimum power the Soviet Union needed to keep its industry going. A Yale University professor, Bernard Brodie, who studied the new set of JCS plans for the air force, concluded that the planners "simply expected the Soviet Union to collapse as a result of the bombing campaign. . . . People kept talking about the 'Sunday Punch.' "

Another strong critic of the Joint Chief's new target demands was General LeMay himself. He complained bitterly that some of the targets, if and when they were actually placed on the map, would be in areas unfamiliar to the aircrews and, therefore, hard to find and, because they were not near large cities, the "bonus damage" factor would be severely reduced. He argued for a return to the urban-industrial targets and he won a major concession from the Joint Chiefs' target panel. They agreed, in future, to submit target lists to SAC for comment before sending them for final approval to the JCS. LeMay had more victories on the way. A few months later the air force consolidated its influence over the target selection process by removing the army and navy from effective participation. When the army general Dwight Eisenhower moved into the White House in January 1953, Curtis LeMay was driving the numbers in the stockpile ever upward. Very soon he was to gain custody of complete bombs as well.

3

The Vacuum Cleaner

FROM a distance, all you can see of Diogenes Station are two huge, white, golfball-shaped objects lodged on the side of a barren, rocky hillside that slopes gently down to the southern shore of the Black Sea. The balls are the protective covers for radar dishes, antennae, and a host of electronic equipment used by America to spy on the Soviet Union. It is a bleak spot. The nearest town is Sinop, 350 miles from Istanbul east along the Black Sea coastal road. To the north, 200 across the sea, lies the Soviet port of Sevastopol, and approximately 600 miles to the northeast is one of the first Soviet missile testing stations at Kapustin Yar.

A contingent of 450 U.S. Army and Air Force intelligence specialists live in the small compound at Sinop, a self-contained little America with a bowling alley, a laundromat, and a hi-fi club. It is a hardship post: Supplies of water and electricity are erratic, the sewage system has a nasty habit of breaking down, and the services are as unpredictable as the military dictatorship that rules the country. The Turkish flag flies over the compound as a symbol of Turkish "control" over Diogenes Station and a gesture of friendliness to the Turkish "commander," but this is strictly an American operation. The radars and the antennae are manned twenty-four hours a day, monitoring anything from a telephone call to a rocket launch on the other side of the water. The "cryppies," as the people who work in the cryptology branch are known, try to ignore their unenviable position as pawns in on-again-off-again U.S.-Turkish relations; for the most part, they are dedicated soldiers, convinced that their work is critical to national security and willing to rough it at Sinop for twelve months—the minimum tour of duty.

The base was set up in the late 1950s, almost immediately after the Soviets started testing rockets at Kapustin Yar. The primary mission is the same today as it was then: to collect "strategic intelligence," information that will give analysts in Washington long-range indications of the possibility and nature of hostile actions. It is the I of C-cubed-I and includes monitoring signals intelligence (SIGINT) on Soviet military and political developments and recording missile telemetry data, which are transmitted by the rocket during flight to monitors on the ground that record exactly how the test is going.

When on duty at Diogenes Station the soldiers are said to be "sitting position." They rotate on three eight-hour shifts, operating some of the most sophisticated electronic bugs in the world. Most of the operators hold an intelligence service rank called "98G." They are communications intelligence (COMINT) intercept specialists, Russian linguists who spend their shift time listening to the known frequencies of Soviet military and government communications and transcribing or recording those communications considered to be of any intelligence value. Theirs is a working day of "spot reports," of the movement, perhaps, of an infantry battalion or a military exercise, and "tip-offs," alerting other collectors of something unusual or unexpected. For the most part they monitor messages that are either sent uncoded—"in the clear"—or put into known, low-level classification codes.

Also "sitting position" at Diogenes are a smaller number of operators with the rank of "98J." They are electronic intelligence (ELINT) specialists. Unlike the COMINT operators who deal with voice or wire communications, the ELINT specialists spend their time in front of TV screens looking for "emanations," electronic pulses from radar sites along the Soviet border, from ships and from aircraft. On the Soviet north coast of the Black Sea, for example, there are scores of surface-to-air defense missile sites, each of which has two radars, one for searching for enemy planes in the sky to the south and one for guiding the missile to its target. When the radars are switched on, during a test or a military operation, they emit pulses of energy at regular intervals and at a specific frequency. Each radar type has its own "signature," occupying a special position in the frequency band much like a radio station. The ELINT specialists catalog the emanations and compare them with signals listed in the secret bible of known emanating locations, the EOB (electronic order of battle). When a new signal, either a radio frequency (RF) or a pulse repetition frequency (PRF), is discovered the information is sent back to Washington for special analysis and is eventually included in a comprehensive survey of

Soviet air defenses used by U.S. bombers. Most of the work for the 98Gs and 98Js is dull, routine stuff. But occasionally the 98Js catch a "big one," a Soviet missile test. Then, instead of collecting ELINT, they put on their TELINT hats, tracking and "listening in" on the fifty or so channels of missile telemetry until the missile goes off their screens and is picked up by another station like Diogenes in Alaska.

Diogenes is one of several eavesdropping posts that have ringed the Soviet Union for more than twenty years. Some are located at equally remote and unfamiliar spots —Sebana Seca in Puerto Rico, Pyongtaek in Korea, Pine Gap in Australia, Misawa in Japan, Chicksands in England. Others sit conspicuously out of place in the middle of cities, like Teufelsberg in West Berlin, perched on a hill made from the rubble of World War II. The bases are officially described as being involved in "radio research," "atmospheric and phenomenological studies," "space research," and "geophysical research," but they are all part of the largest spy network in the world.

In the age of spy satellites that can pick out a man from 300 miles above the earth's surface, the eavesdropper's art is becoming increasingly crude and imprecise by comparison. Indeed, bases such as Diogenes Station are facing the budget ax, not because of any fundamental change in the need for their information, but because their large manpower requirements make them so much more expensive to operate than an object in space. COMINT and ELINT specialists can now "sit position" at the U.S. Defense Department's Special Missile and Aeronautics Center ("deaf-smack" as it is known) in a Washington, D.C., suburb and eavesdrop on the same conversations that are picked up by satellites.

That is not to say that all such stations are totally obsolete. They may still be useful in providing intelligence from parts of the world where satellite coverage is incomplete, or where "communications discipline" is so poor that a ground station, even in an embassy, can have free access to government messages. But the eavesdroppers of Diogenes Station belong to another era, to the decade of the 1950s when the U.S. policy of containing the Soviet Union required an ever-tightening noose of medium-range nuclear forces around the borders of the U.S.S.R. and when General Curtis LeMay and his SAC aircrews were desperate for any tidbit of intelligence that would help them identify another airfield, radar site, or other new military target. That was when human beings still played the leading role in intelligence collection. They sat on the edges of mountains in remote, unheard-of places; they made daring forays behind enemy lines; and they flew uncomfortably high in strange-looking aircraft searching for targets and signs that the Soviet Union was preparing to make nuclear war against the United States.

The fledgling postwar intelligence-gathering apparatus expanded rapidly and by the late 1950s two basic types of intelligence had been identified: strategic, or long-range, such as that gathered at Diogenes Station, and early warning, or tactical warning, such as that gathered by the ring of radar sites strung along the north of the American continent. It is convenient to separate the two historically: Strategic intelligence was the more important in the 1950s when the Soviet Union had few nuclear bombers capable of flying from Russian bases to America and even fewer bombs. What the U.S. war planners wanted to know was exactly how many bombers they had, where the targets were, and how well the enemy could fight back. Only then could they make up their war plans. In the missile age, with the short flight of intercontinental rockets, early warning became even more important.

Because of service and agency rivalries, geographic responsibilities, and bureaucratic requirements, the collection of strategic intelligence was divided among numerous organizations. The CIA, the traditional master spy department operating independently of any other government agency, was forced to share the battlefield with special military units set up to look after their own interests. They were the predecessors of the Electronic Security Command of today's air force, the army's Intelligence and Security Command, and the navy's Security Group. These were the units that actually operated and manned the ground, naval, and air "platforms"—the bases, the ships, and the airplanes that collected the intelligence.

Over the years, the Strategic Air Command became not only a major consumer but also a dominant, if largely unnoticed, operator in strategic intelligence. The commanders of SAC gradually edged their way into the collection process so that by the end of the 1970s they had a hand in virtually all intelligence operations, both strategic and early warning, that in any way related to nuclear attack or defense of the United States. It was not just a bureaucratic takeover where the agency most concerned did most of the work; it was a conscious and determined effort to restructure the collection of intelligence so that it satisfied one main aim—the preparation and implementation of the SIOP. The compression of both warning and reaction time of nuclear attack dictated this change in the traditional function of intelligence gathering: The aim now was to provide intelligence on enemy activity that could be used in a board range of military and political moves.

At first, thirst for information in the new "denied areas" of the Soviet Union in the immediate postwar years spawned a number of enterprising, and largely uncoordinated, projects that did not involve the Strategic Air Command. There was Project Wringer, a huge program in Germany, Austria, and Japan designed, quite literally, to wring information from the thousands of prisoners of war repatriated from the Soviet Union. In fact, most of SAC's basic intelligence on the Soviet Union in the period 1949–53 came from Project Wringer. Special missions of air force bombers and transport planes, plus navy patrol planes, were sent to look for Soviet radar sites and military bases, and, starting in 1950, specially equipped reconnaissance aircraft belonging to SAC, the RB-36 and the RB-50, were flying missions along the Soviet borders, and a few actually crossed into Soviet territory.

Occasionally, the CIA would become involved, sending agents into such places as the Ukraine to check on the status of an airfield or a known military installation. The CIA was also fond of dreaming up its own special tricks. One, code named "Moby Dick," consisted of a string of high-flying balloons with cameras attached that were sent drifting on the prevailing surface winds across the Soviet Union from Western Europe to Japan. Some of the balloons were actually recovered, but because it was not possible to track the balloons in flight it was also not possible to know the location of the photographs taken. It was, however, always obvious that if any good intelligence was ever to be gleaned from inside the new Russia it would have to come from the air, as the history of intelligence collection made clear.

The earliest recorded aerial reconnaissance mission was in 1794 by a French army officer, Captain J. M. J. Coutelle, who flew tethered manned balloons above enemy positions during the French revolutionary wars. Baffled by the aerial observation, the soldiers in their brightly colored uniforms made no attempt to camouflage themselves or avoid detection. With the introduction of powered military flight, observation was no longer restricted by the length of the tethering cable, and an airplane could search out the enemy and follow troop movements, roaming deep into enemy territory. The first recorded use of a reconnaissance airplane in war was in October 1911, when a Captain Piazza of the Italian army air detachment flew his monoplane over the Tripoli area to reconnoiter the Ottoman positions. In later flights he had a hand-held camera and took pictures of the Turkish troops.

By the beginning of World War I, all of the major combatants had reconnaissance aircraft, and one of the reasons combat aircraft evolved so rapidly was the need to shoot down these spies in the sky. The actual success of aerial espionage was still limited, however, largely because of poor maps. Many pilots got lost and invariably gave erroneous geographic references of enemy troop movements. Even the best pilots, flying the unstable aircraft while simultaneously taking photographs or making sketches and notes, had an almost impossible task. Vertical objects are not easily identifiable from hundreds of feet in the air, and light can play strange tricks on an observer. A story, perhaps apocryphal, from the early reconnaissance days tells of a pilot who mistook the evenly spaced shadows cast by tombstones in a cemetery for a military encampment.

The development of a lightweight, air-to-ground radio was to have a dramatic effect on the pilot's ability to report effectively what he saw, and to direct artillery fire on enemy positions. The early wireless radios weighed over 100 pounds and were so bulky that, in the new two-seaters, the observer had to be removed in favor of the equipment. But, by the end of 1915, radios weighing under 20 pounds and fitting neatly underneath the cockpit instrument panel allowed an observer to be reinstated and to maintain "real-time" contact with the ground. This also allowed information on the enemy to be observed and transmitted to headquarters at approximately the same time. By the end of the war, air reconnaissance was, in the words of the official history of the Royal Flying Corps, "routine insurance against surprise." It was also becoming a major source of information on the enemy's order of battle. Thousands of aerial photographs were being taken of troop dispositions, movements, and fortifications. It is hard to imagine today how primitive these cameras were, strapped to the side of the planes with photographic plates and precarious exposure mechanisms. Once developed, the photograph lacked definition: It was impossible in a photograph taken from, say, 3,000 feet, the normal operating height, to detect a soldier standing in a field.

Today, satellites orbiting the earth at a height of 300 miles not only can pick out a man, but can also show whether he is carrying a gun. As the reconnaissance techniques became more sophisticated, nations began to realize that they had to protect their own airspace—even in peacetime—from the airborne spies. Overflights were restricted to certain air corridors. In the late 1930s, the French and the British, using regular commercial aircraft fitted with hidden cameras, ran the first covert reconnaissance missions to photograph the German military buildup. During the Second World War, air reconnaissance, on both sides, was a major part of the air forces' operations. But for all their daring exploits, the pilots brought back only a fraction of the information that reconnaissance equipment on today's spy planes and satellites delivers in a week.

The introduction of jet aircraft with their greater speed and maneuverability invited huge advances in camera techniques and film speed. The photographic industry obliged and the quality of the photographs improved enormously. During the "limited conflict" in Korea, where it became vital to identify the enemy precisely, the value of photographic reconnaissance began to impress the politicians. President Eisenhower, long an admirer of aerial spying, was faced with a continuing poor intelligence of the Soviet Union's emerging atomic capability so he proposed an "open skies" plan at the 1955 Geneva summit conference. The United States and the Soviet Union, he suggested, should provide aerial photography facilities to each other and thus the increasing mistrust between the two could be removed. The proposal was largely a political ploy, however, and it is not hard to understand why the Soviet Union could not accept the Eisenhower plan: It was almost totally to America's advantage. The United States may have known little of the Soviet interior, especially of Soviet nuclear developments, yet many key items of strategic intelligence value about America's military the Russians could read in the American press.

The Soviets rejected the plan on the mistaken belief that parts of their territory would always remain outside the scope of the American spy planes and listening posts. They believed, in the words of Marshall Nikolai Bulganin, then Soviet premier, that "both countries stretch over vast territories in which, if one desired, one could conceal anything." By the late 1950s the era of ELINT and COMINT had arrived; the Soviet Union was surrounded by a web of eavesdroppers—and the Americans had more tricks up their sleeves.

ELINT operations provided crucial information for the program of limited overflights by RAF Canberras, modified B-29 bombers, and RB-47 jets along the periphery of the Soviet Union. These were short-range missions designed to ferret out the Soviet air defenses. The ELINT pinpointed the radar sites and the air defense artillery batteries, information that would ultimately go into the target folders of attacking American bombers. But in the long run these flights were counterproductive because they gave the Soviets regular, and real, training in air defense and accelerated the Soviet missile research. The CIA's unmanned reconnaissance balloons were still operating, but they were increasingly useless because Soviet fighters had started shooting them down before they reached Japanese airspace. For a brief period around 1954 all reconnaissance flights were discontinued because they were becoming a political embarrassment.

The problem of collecting Soviet intelligence remained, however. In fact, information about the Soviet missile developments was so poor that it was impossible to make reasonable judgments as to whether the U.S. bomber force was becoming vulnerable to missile attack. The highest-level intelligence requirement of the Cold War was to collect information on the new long-range missile targets deep inside the Soviet Union, to the east of the Ural Mountains, where Soviet research and testing centers had been established away from the more vulnerable and populated Ukraine. To reach these sites the Americans would require something better than a modified B-29 bomber rigged with cameras and bristling with antennae. In 1956, the United States embarked on the most daring, most successful, and, finally, the most disastrous of all aerial reconnaissance missions against the Soviet Union: Operation Overflight, the deep penetration of Soviet airspace by America's new superspy plane, the U-2.

The job of building a new high-altitude plane capable of flying well above the range of the Soviet fighters and air defenses was given to the CIA. For the moment the most secret and sensitive covert operations in intelligence gathering were still being assigned to the civilian experts. With extraordinary speed one of Lockheed's foremost designers, Clarence L. "Kelly" Johnson, turned out a prototype U-2 in a secret workshop near Burbank, California. The plane made its maiden flight only eight months after the decision had been made to build it. Everything about the U-2 was top secret; it carried no exterior markings and even its official designation was "U" for utility, rather than the traditional "R" for reconnaissance. In keeping with its sinister role, the pilots nicknamed the plane the Black Widow.

It was a distinctive, bizarre-looking craft. Its thin 103-foot-long wings were almost twice as long as its 63-foot-fuselage; it looked more like a glider than a regular jet. Its performance was remarkable. It could fly at more than 70,000 feet, twice the altitude that jets of the day could reach, and it could carry enough fuel for more than ten hours of flight. It was not an easy plane to fly, however, because the delicate airframe could not withstand any sharp maneuvers. Flying at such high altitudes also meant added discomforts for the pilot. Each flight began with a special session in a pressure chamber during which the pilot was put on pure oxygen for two hours to eliminate as much nitrogen as possible from his bloodstream. An excess of nitrogen, a common symptom of high flyers and deep divers, causes dizziness and eventually blackout, commonly known as "the bends." The pilots had to wear a special pressure suit and gloves and the long flights in the cramped cockpits were extremely tiring and uncomfortable. Only low-residue foods, such as steak and eggs, were eaten before missions, but that did not always solve the toilet problem.

The U-2 flies slowly, at about four hundred miles an hour; it stalls easily; and if it enters a spin after the stall the plane becomes unmanageable, unlike a regular plane in which spins can be controlled. Only the best pilots were chosen, but the accident rate was still high.

When the U-2 missions began in 1956 three groups of U-2s were deployed to overseas bases at Lakenheath in

England, Incirlik in Turkey, and Atsugi in Japan. From these bases almost the entire landmass of the Soviet Union could be covered, but the problem was navigation. The U-2 pilots could not afford to communicate with any Western bases during their flights because that would have revealed their position to Soviet air defenses. They found their way mostly by obtaining fixes on the beams of known Soviet radio stations. But even that procedure had its built-in hazard; the maps of the Soviet Union supplied by the CIA were still extremely poor so that collecting raw geographical data for updating maps was also a regular part of the missions. The U-2s brought back literally thousands of pictures of new potential targets for SAC bombers —military bases, industrial plants, roads, and railways. SAC's target list grew considerably as a result of the missions.

The most important role for the U-2 was spotting the new missile sites and helping the TELINT specialists at Diogenes Station in Sinop and at other bases in Turkey collect telemetry from Soviet missile tests. The photographs taken by the U-2 were of excellent quality thanks to some advanced camera equipment devised by Edwin Land, the ingenious inventor of the Polaroid camera. Land's wide-angle-lens cameras could carry 4,000 frames of film, which enabled the photographing of huge expanses of Soviet territory in one trip. Using seven apertures the cameras were able to photograph a 125-mile strip of land in one frame. Stories abound of how the CIA tried to impress Eisenhower about the U-2's remarkable technology. The CIA is said to have shown Eisenhower pictures of his favorite golf course at Augusta taken from

10,000 feet and Eisenhower reportedly picked out a golf ball. Under ideal conditions, on a clear, cold day with plenty of light, a trained photo-interpreter might be able to accomplish such a feat, but the Eisenhower story is most likely a publicity stunt to justify the risks of the program.

At the same time, the intelligence being picked up by the ring of eavesdropping stations was so good that the U-2 squadrons often had several days' advance warning of a missile test. The problem was that the test sites were being moved increasingly farther away from the U-2 bases; the first experimental Soviet intercontinental missiles were fired from test beds at Tyuratam in Kazakhstan, at least 1,500 miles from the U-2 base in Turkey.

Between 1956 and 1958 about twenty "deep penetration" missions were carried out and, despite the top secret classification on all of them, some informed speculation about the U-2's real role began to leak to the technical press and eventually to the *New York Times*. The publicity caused problems. The British and German governments requested that the planes not use their bases and most of the U-2s ended up in Turkey. A few flights took place out of temporary facilities at Lahore and Peshawar in Pakistan and at Bodo in Norway, at bases in Taiwan, and at other secret bases. As the number of sites allowing U-2 operations declined, however, the need for the missions also became more acute. On 26 August 1957 the Soviets launched their first successful intercontinental missile, and on 4 October of that same year shocked the Western world by sending *Sputnik* into orbit around the earth.

By 1959, the U-2 pilots, using their increasingly sophis-ticated electronic equipment, discovered that the Soviets were regularly tracking their flights and were also making some valiant efforts at shooting them down. Because of the higher risks, the flights were briefly curtailed, but in May 1960 two missions were scheduled from Peshawar, in Pakistan, across the Soviet Union to Norway. It was the first time a U-2 would fly from south to north across Soviet territory. One of the pilots was a former air force lieuten-ant, Francis Gary Powers, a 32-year-old Virginian who had flown U-2 missions from the beginning and was con-sidered one of the CIA's best pilots. Suspecting that the Soviets were about to deploy their first intercontinental missile, the CIA was determined to schedule more U-2 flights and cover as many targets as possible. Powers's flight plan took him deeper into Soviet territory than any U-2 had ever been.

Presidential approval for the flight was obtained min-utes before Powers was due to take off on May Day 1960. The route went directly over the Tyuratam test center, north to Sverdlovsk, known to house atomic energy plants, and on to Plesetsk where operational ICBM silos for the SS-6 missile were thought to be under construction. A few hours into his mission Powers was shot down by an SA-2 missile fired from a Soviet airfield not marked on his map. The SA-2 hit the plane at a height of thirteen miles. Powers bailed out and was captured, and an embarrassing show trial took place in Moscow. Powers was sentenced to ten years for espionage but was exchanged for a Soviet spy two years later. Operation Overflight came to an abrupt end, but Allen Dulles, then CIA director, later observed

that the U-2 missions were the most useful intelligence
tools of the 1950s.

After the end of Operation Overflight, military leaders,
always angered by the CIA's interference in their affairs by
its control of the U-2 missions, seized their chance and
moved swiftly to "correct" the matter. The military side
of intelligence gathering was proliferating to such an extent during the early 1950s that the Pentagon chiefs easily
justified taking military intelligence collection operations
out of the CIA's bailiwick. At the same time they decided
to divide up control of intelligence operations between
two new superagencies: SAC was given responsibility for
strategic aerial reconnaissance, and the National Security
Agency (NSA), had responsibility for all signals intelligence.

SAC's aerial reconnaissance empire would swiftly annex
the U-2 program and add it to a growing stable of spy
planes. Before the U-2 overflights came to an end, another, equally impressive reconnaissance aircraft was on
the drawing board. Known as the SR-71, the new plane
could fly faster and higher than any other plane. Its operational speed at 80,000 feet was three times the speed of
sound. First deployed in 1966, the SR-71, nicknamed the
Blackbird, would share reconnaissance duties with the
U-2. Able to go higher, the SR-71 could quickly survey vast
expanses of territory, leaving the slower U-2 to pick out
the details. Another spy plane, the RC-135, a converted
Boeing 707 crammed with radar gear, listening equipment, and twenty-five technicians, was virtually a flying
SIGINT station. The RC-135 was the intermediate stage

between ground stations and satellites. Reflecting the exploratory nature of their mission the planes had code names like "Big Safari" and "Covered Wagon."

The routes and targets of the reconnaissance planes are all controlled now by the JCS, and the information is analyzed by the NSA. The planes fly out of Athens (Hellenikon Air Base) in Greece, Mildenhall in England, Akrotiri in Cyrpus, Osan in South Korea, Guam, Hawaii, Okinawa, and Alaska. They also sometimes operate secretly out of bases in Egypt, Turkey, Pakistan, and Thailand. The SIGINT aircraft, with translators and decoders aboard, fly regular "tracks" along the borders of the Soviet Union and East European countries, as well as over Asian, African, Middle Eastern, and Latin American allies and adversaries.

In 1952, the National Security Agency was set up by the secretary of defense and charged with the responsibility of consolidating the signals intelligence of the three armed services. It was given complete operational control over the network of eavesdropping posts around the world and ultimate authority over anything to do with codes, cryptography, and communications security. Moreover, NSA, acting either together with the CIA or alone, operated intelligence collection stations that were not part of the military network. Since then these have included politically sensitive locations in Pakistan, Iran, China, Norway, Taiwan, and Australia. Communications intercept operations were also expanded in American embassies and consulates abroad, and an entirely new, supersecret ring of covert foreign cells was opened up. These cells were "compartmented"; that is, knowledge about them and information derived from them were severely restricted. Politically sensitive phone-tapping and code-breaking operations were particularly closely held and access to the information was not regularly available to the military or to SAC targeteers on a day-to-day basis.

A large amount of information was also obtained through close collaboration among trusted allies, the so-called ABCA countries—America, Britain, Canada, and Australia. From the beginning, British SIGINT operators manned the stations jointly with Americans. The old outposts of the Empire gave the British something to trade for the Americans' ever-increasingly superior espionage network and technology. British SIGINT sites already operating in places like Hong Kong and Singapore were valuable extensions of the American network. Today these sites intercept voice communications, radar, and electronic signals and conduct analyses of troop movements. There are now about twenty-five major listening stations, among them Berlin and Augsburg in Germany; Chicksands in England; Edzell in Scotland; San Vito dei Normanni, near Brindisi, in Italy; Sinop in Turkey; Diego Garcia in the Indian Ocean; Pyongtaek and Osan in Korea; Sobe and Misawa in Japan; Sebana Seca in Puerto Rico; and Panama.

Information from the listening stations and reconnaissance aircraft became known as "special intelligence," or SI. This information has always been kept separate from other military intelligence operations. Those involved in SI work require stiffer background investigations and higher classification clearances and are considered, or at least consider themselves, the elite of the United States intelligence community.

That community now employs about 25,000 people at various headquarters in or near Washington, D.C., and more than 100,000 worldwide. Their funding is hidden in line items in the Defense Department budget under headings like "special activities," "special programs," and "special update programs." The total is more than $13 billion a year, with another $10 billion spent on reconnaissance, early warning, base maintenance, and personnel. The community is directed from little-known intelligence command posts: the Strategic Reconnaissance Center of the Joint Chiefs of Staff in the Pentagon; the National Military Intelligence Center of the Defense Intelligence Agency, also in the Pentagon; the National SIGINT Operations Center of the NSA, at Fort Meade, Maryland; and the CIA Operations Center at Langley, Virginia.

Until the mid-1970s, the high classification and restrictions on SI operations meant that NSA had complete control of the information. SI restrictions insulated the information and operations from the tactical and war-fighting concerns of SAC and others. Slowly, however, the SAC planners and the new strategic C³I specialists, with their insatiable appetites for intelligence information relating to nuclear war plans, have opened the doors to the SI operations. It is no coincidence that in the process SAC acquired a greater hand in almost every aspect of intelligence and therefore could exercise a greater degree of control over target selection, bomb requirements, and the conduct of nuclear war.

4
The Defenders

AMERICANS have never really recovered from the deep psychological blow of being beaten into space by the Russians. It happened on 4 October 1957, when a small ball of technical tricks known as *Sputnik I* bleeped its way around the earth while the world gawked incredulously. A quarter of a century later, in 1982, Americans still remembered how it had been. "It was Us versus Them," wrote one columnist in the *Washington Post;* "it was the American way of life, not to mention tail fins, Wrigley's Spearmint gum, Wednesday night bowling and attending the church of your choice, going against the godless horde." The Russian triumph "hit where it hurt," recalled another columnist; *"Sputnik* ended once and for all the American assumption that the Soviets wrapped their heads in bags and worked in factories making lousy shoes that wore out in three months." Indeed, across the nation anger and frustration at *Sputnik* were so prevalent that, if President Eisenhower had volunteered to get back at the Russians by firing himself into space, Americans probably would have agreed.

In a desperate effort to recover their technological balance, the Americans invented the race to the moon—and won. It was a civilian propaganda exercise, brilliantly conceived and brilliantly executed. Behind the moon race, however, was a military space race that was bigger, more expensive, and very secret. American pride may have taken a fall when *Sputnik I* went into orbit, but to the war planners *Sputnik* meant intercontinental missiles, which were then hailed as "the ultimate weapon." The arithmetic of nuclear war suddenly changed in a terrifying way: the time between the first sighting of a nuclear attack launched by the Soviet Union to the moment it landed on American soil evaporated from a relatively comfortable eight hours to just under twenty-five minutes.

To be sure, there were some in the U.S. Air Force, especially the Luddites of the bomber age, who smugly dismissed those who were in a panic about the immediate safety of the free world. "Technical studies completed during the year," the chief of staff of the air force wrote in his 1957 annual report, "confirmed the reasonable expectation that before too long it will be possible to produce devices capable of destroying missiles in flight."

Such embarrassing predictions were quickly buried by the difficulties in and enormous costs of developing antimissile missiles, however, and the U.S. embarked on a huge program of top secret space enterprises, laying the foundations of a spy satellite and early-warning system that would become an integral part of the SIOP. The military space program forged ahead, some of it so secret that for many years the air force refused to acknowledge the existence of many of the most important programs. By the beginning of the 1980s, the National Aeronautics and Space Administration's exciting civilian adventures into space—to Mars, Venus, Saturn, and Jupiter—had been drastically cut for cost reasons. American priorities were now different: For the first time, the budget for military applications in outer space exceeded the civilian one. The question of how mankind would avoid space wars between the two superpowers enthralled a few defense intellectuals, but it was a distant, futuristic worry compared to the possibility of the "Earth war" that still loomed. The huge sums that America spent on early-warning systems and satellite detection were sold to the public as necessary not only for the defense of the West, but also as a means of helping to *prevent* a nuclear war that might happen through accidental firing of a nuclear weapon. But unwitting American taxpayers got more than they knew about in the "defense" packages of the last twenty years. They "bought" a system of detecting missiles and nuclear explosions that became part of a nuclear arsenal designed to *fight* a nuclear war. In that case the "defenders" could also be the "attackers."

The panic about America's security in the nuclear age had started well before *Sputnik*. The Russians had embarrassed the American defense establishment once before, in 1949, by exploding their first atomic device several years ahead of Western estimates. The reaction had been no less dramatic. Many American policymakers were convinced that the Russians would stop at nothing to use nuclear weapons against the United States, even to the extent of sending "kamikaze" bombers on one-way missions. Now that the U.S. was no longer insulated by virtue of its geography from Soviet long-range bombers, these policymakers believed that a bomber defense and early-warning system had to be built. Few stopped to ask whether the Russians, desperately trying to recover from the ravages of war, would not consider an attack on the U.S. to be foolish beyond even their own paranoid reasoning. A system of "continental air defense" became one of the major concerns of the early Cold War.

Mistrust of the Russians was such that an air defense system was identified as the country's "most urgent" requirement in the first report of the newly established Defense Department in 1947. "The lack today of an adequate radar warning and control system remains one of the most serious deficiencies in providing for our national security," declared the report. At the newly established Air Force Department, General Hoyt Vandenberg, air force vice chief of staff, led a campaign to create a more effective system of detecting and shooting down Soviet bombers. *Defense,* he maintained, was just as crucial to the nation's security as SAC's growing offensive nuclear-strike forces. With Pearl Harbor still uppermost in the collective memory, Vandenberg found many allies for his early-warning net, but postwar military budgets were sparse and the competition was tough—from the occupations in Europe and Japan and, of course, Strategic Air Command.

In the early budget races, the air force "defenders" like Vandenberg lost out time and again to General LeMay's "attackers." Nevertheless, the defenders produced a stream of million dollar "minimum systems" and "emergency coverage" proposals to close the threats from the nonexistent "bomber gap," and some were funded. The groundswell of their efforts spread across the nation, enabling the air force to persuade a large number of suitably frightened citizens to join an all-volunteer reconnaissance force, known as the Ground Observer Corps. These highly motivated people, some 300,000 strong, started "Operation Skywatch" on 14 July 1952, manning more than 10,000 observation posts, some on a 24-hour basis, to watch for low-flying Soviet aircraft slipping under the rudimentary radar net. At its peak, in 1957, the Corps operated in 48 states with a peacetime army of 387,000 "regulars" and 170,000 "reservists" whose 19,000 observation posts ranged from lighthouses to the rooftops of private homes.

As Soviet military power increased, the U.S. air defenses soon contained much more than a few battalions of nuclear bird-watchers. The technological advances included a bomber defense radar screen that was fed information by hundreds of land-based stations, navy radar ships, submarine listening posts, and offshore radar platforms, just like offshore drilling rigs, called Texas Towers. Airborne early-warning aircraft flew round-the-clock missions and, when the weather was fine and the winds were low, the navy flew an early-warning airship, the ZPG-2. Behind the rows of radar detectors a huge force of fighter interceptor aircraft, totaling 2,600 at its peak, stood ready to scramble against any invader. Hundreds of anti-aircraft and air defense missile batteries dotted the land. The cost of this system was rapidly becoming billions, not millions, of dollars in the annual U.S. budget.

A new military concept of "defense in depth" was born. By 1953, a continuous radar net was operating throughout the United States, extending into Alaska, across northern

Canada to Newfoundland, Labrador, and Greenland, and across the sea to Iceland. Three new radar fences were built across the top of the North American landmass. The Pine Tree Line, the southernmost of the three, skirted the Canadian-American border, literally within the pine forests. The middle line, built mostly to the north of settled territory, hugged the 55th parallel. The third line, dubbed the Dew Line, for Distant Early Warning Line, was much farther north and the most ambitious of the radar fences. It was also the most expensive to construct, at over $500 million.

When the main section was complete in 1957, the Dew Line increased the advanced warning of incoming bombers by three hours, from five to eight. Located within the Arctic Circle the Dew Line was able to detect aircraft coming toward the North American continent from over the North Pole. During its construction, workers and equipment had to be moved into the frozen Canadian northern wilderness. One hundred ships were needed to carry the 50,000 tons of cargo and the three million barrels of oil needed to build and supply the thirty-one stations. The first and main segment—from Cape Lisburne, Alaska, to Cape Dyer, Baffin Island—was completed in 1957. The final stage, in Iceland, was finished in 1962.

The Pentagon now had an unbroken, 6,000-mile radar fence from the Aleutians to the middle of the Atlantic Ocean. The eight-hour warning time was enough to ensure that the nuclear war plans of SAC could be executed and that their bombers would be airborne long before an attack on the bases. Information from these radar stations was fed into the new North American Aerospace Defense Command (NORAD) at an air base at Colorado Springs in the foothills of the southern Rocky Mountains. In the early 1960s the command post was buried in a hollowed-out granite mountain (Cheyenne Mountain) in the Rockies. In those days of less accurate missiles, it was considered bombproof.

Processing large amounts of data from the radar early-warning system required a new electronic device that could not only determine the speed and altitude but also predict and report the course of hundreds of aircraft and quickly give that information to the interceptors and missiles. Moreover, the air force needed all these computations in a fraction of a second. They found such a marvel in a "computer" called the Semi-Automatic Ground Environment, with an apt acronym, SAGE. The Pentagon said it was an "automatic brain," something that would be safe and efficient because it "removed the human element by replacing man with automatic equipment."

Meanwhile, the radars themselves got bigger and bigger. Huge radar dishes, some as big as football fields, were built at northern stations to cover the approaches over the North Pole. They scanned the skies, not so much for bombers now, but for the emerging Soviet missile force. Three of the largest radar stations, called the Ballistic Missile Early Warning System, or BMEWS, were built at Clear in Alaska, Thule in Greenland, and Fylingdales Moor in Yorkshire. This last site, a joint U.S.-British project, began scanning the northern skies in September 1963. For all practical purposes this early-warning network eliminated any prospects of a surprise attack. The new nuclear commanders received their instant, computerized information in their underground bunkers at NORAD and at the SAC command post at Offutt Air Force

Base, near Omaha. Yet for all the money spent on the air defense system, it had been beaten by the new technology of intercontinental missiles. The missiles could fly in minutes the thousands of miles the bombers covered in hours; the billions of dollars had bought no additional time for the man in the White House. And although the "defenders" were about to spend billions more on even more expensive satellites to "improve" the early-warning system, they could never increase the amount of decision time.

In vaulted offices on the fourth floor of the Pentagon, the air force officers in charge of satellite intelligence collection went to great lengths to obscure their activities. When they opened their doors in the late 1950s, they worked officially in the "Special Activities Office" and their business was dealing in "national technical means." Actually, they ran the "National Reconnaissance Office," the headquarters of American covert satellite and aerial spying. Jointly with the CIA and the National Security Agency, they supervised the collection and collation of all signals and photographic intelligence picked up, first by the U-2 program and subsequently by America's satellites. Their obsession about secrecy was reinforced in 1960 by the U-2 fiasco, and they were determined not to be caught out again. So tight was the security in the Special Activities Office that prior to 1977 the United States never even acknowledged officially that it had any reconnaissance satellites.

In fact, a secret satellite program was already under way at the time of *Sputnik I*. In 1956 the air force had given Lockheed a contract to design a satellite that could take pictures of the earth and send them back in a tiny capsule that would float down to earth by parachute. It was hoped that the capsule would land in the sea where it could be scooped up by the navy. *Sputnik* and the U-2 affair gave a tremendous boost to the military space program, and funding was quadrupled.

Three new military satellite programs emerged. The first project was hidden in an otherwise well-publicized "research" program known as Discoverer. The second was a reconnaissance project called Sentry (later changed to SAMOS, standing for Satellite and Missile Observation System). The third, and most secret of all, was MIDAS, the Missile Detection Alarm System, a satellite to detect the actual launch of a missile through the heat of its exhaust acting on the satellite's infrared sensors.

There were many initial problems, however. The first launch of a Discoverer spacecraft from Vandenburg Air Force Base in California in February 1959 was a flop; it failed to complete its first orbit. The program was not a complete success until August 1960, when Discoverer No. 14 circled the earth three times, passing right over the Soviet Union, took some pictures, and fell back to earth. The film capsule was recovered from the Pacific Ocean south of Hawaii.

In addition to the somewhat difficult method of finding small packets of film in the middle of the ocean, a second way of retrieving the information was by using radio relays. A tape machine on board the satellite would film selected locations on earth and later "dump" the information into an earth station receiver as it passed overhead. In the early days, this method was more reliable than ocean capsules, and it also ensured almost instantaneous reception, but the pictures were of poorer quality. The radio relays used in the SAMOS satellites were found to be useful for identifying military bases and topography, but insufficient for detailed technical analyses of Soviet missiles or other weaponry. The air force was still concerned mainly with collecting target data so the SAMOS pictures suited them fine. The CIA, on other hand, was more interested in the better definition provided by the film actually returned in the ocean capsules, and they devised a special means of recovery—scooping up the still-falling capsule in large nets attached to slow-flying aircraft. In case the midair snatch proved fruitless, as it did more often than not initially, navy frogmen were always on hand to dive for it.

The first completely successful SAMOS spy satellite launch was on 31 January 1961 from Point Arguello, California. For twenty days it orbited the earth, passing over the Soviet Union seven times a day and radioing enough information back to ground stations to "inventory Soviet ICBM strength," according to one study. SAMOS radioed pictures back to the ground stations using an ingenious new system. After the satellite had taken a picture with normal film, it was automatically developed on board and the negative was scanned by a pinpoint ray of light that generated an electrical signal proportional to the intensity of the image on the negative. The signal was then amplified and transmitted to earth where it was fed into a machine that reproduced the image. The light ray moved across the negative in a set pattern covering the 2.5-inch-wide film strip with 17,000 horizontal scans until the whole picture was covered.

By 1963 the satellite spies were being successfully launched on a regular basis, but the results were spasmodic. Sometimes there were too many clouds obscuring the "target" areas, and much of the intelligence was "negative"—the only thing it proved was that there were no missiles or bombers in the area covered by the satellite. Nevertheless, satellite surveillance opened up the Soviet landmass once again to American electronic eyes, and more realistic estimates could be made of the progress of the Soviet weapons programs. Rumors of a missile gap were finally buried once information from SAMOS and Discoverer started pouring in. And analysis of the extent and progress of Soviet missile developments was now possible from this new information source.

The Pentagon's "Special Activities Office" was pressured to find ways to improve the early warning of an attack from the emerging Soviet intercontinental missile force. One possible way was through the MIDAS satellite program. In theory, the alarm would go off as soon as a rocket was launched. But the MIDAS concept proved the most difficult of all the reconnaissance projects to perfect. Orbiting satellites normally spin, but the special infrared sensors, made by the International Telephone and Telegraph Company, could pick up the heat "signal" only if the satellite remained stable. The extra equipment needed to produce stability made the satellites much heavier than Discoverer or SAMOS, and too heavy for the launchers of the day. The first MIDAS satellites were tested in 1960, but the program did not become operational until 1972. In the meantime, MIDAS was updated with new satellites, which lost their original identity. MIDAS became Program 461, then Program 266, then Program 949, and finally Program 647L, a suitably anonymous title. For Congressional and public consumption, 647L was known as the Defense Support Program, or DSP. DSP's masters were more determined than ever to hide the project, even to the extent of not mentioning its name. Here is how a 1981 State Department report to Congress describes DSP:

"[Deleted] currently consists of [deleted] satellite; two [deleted] satellites; a [deleted] for [deleted] and the [deleted] satellites; and a [deleted] which provides a [deleted] for the [deleted]."

The DSP consists of three $150 million satellites parked 22,300 miles up in geosynchronous orbit; that is, they orbit the earth at precisely the same speed that the earth is revolving and thus always remain in the same spot. One is positioned over South America, another over the central Pacific, and a third over the Indian Ocean. They are 22 feet long, 9 feet in diameter, and weigh 2,500 pounds. They maintain a constant watch over the Soviet Union, China, and the oceans, and they are designed to provide the first warning of a missile attack, either by land or by sea.

Each satellite has an infrared detecting telescope, some 12 feet long, always pointing down to earth and set at an angle of 7.5 degrees from the body of the satellite. The telescope scans a conical area of the planet below as the satellite spins at a rate of seven turns a minute; a countermotion wheel maintains stability for the telescope. Any infrared energy on the earth's surface within the conical field covered by the telescope is picked up and reflected off a mirror onto a series of 2,000 angled, two-dimensional detector cells made of lead sulfide, a compound that makes the cells highly sensitive to infrared energy. The satellite computes data from the activated cells and is able to report the intensity of the infrared energy and its point of origin on the earth's surface.

Within less than a minute of a missile launch, the satellites can sense the infrared heat from the rocket plume and the burning missile motor—as long as there are no clouds covering the launch site. If there are clouds, the sensors will pick up the motor's heat once the missile has broken through the cloud cover. Information from the satellite is then transmitted to two DSP "readout stations" where the "mission data" are processed and forwarded almost instantaneously to the national command posts on the American continent. The two readout stations are at Buckley Air National Guard Base in Aurora, Colorado, and at Nurrungar in central Australia.

At each readout station the special characteristics of the "mission data" are analyzed by comparing them with a "library" of previous test flights or satellite launches, and an assessment is made as to whether the launch is on a "threat fan," that is, a path ending in the United States or an allied country. All this information is transmitted instantaneously via satellite to the SAC underground command post at Offutt Air Force Base, the NORAD command post in the Rocky Mountains, the National Military Command Center in the Pentagon, and the Alternate National Military Command Center at Raven Rock, Pennsylvania.

Early-warning duty officers in U.S. Air Force radar stations around the world routinely watch every launch of a rocket within the Soviet Union and China and determine whether it is a test, a routine civilian space shot, or a threat. If it appears to be on a threatening course—the military jargon is "threat azimuth"—the warning officers run a sixty-second "confidence rating" check of their sensors and computers to make sure they have not been fooled by them. An accurate "attack assessment" usually takes six minutes from the moment of launch. The DSP satellites detect the launch usually within fifty seconds. The duty officers at the readout stations check their equipment to make sure they have received a genuine alarm and transmit a confirmation of the attack to the national command posts in the U.S. within another ninety seconds. The other warning radars, particularly the BMEWS sites in Alaska, Greenland, and Fylingdales Moor in Yorkshire, make their own confirmations of an attack as soon as the missiles appear on their screens. Once the battle staff in the national command posts has received these confirming messages, known as "dual phenomenology" because the messages are produced from two separate sensors, they hold a telephone conference call known as a "threat assessment conference." This must be concluded within three minutes. There are then nineteen minutes to impact of the missile.

The amount of information available about the incoming missiles is stunning. In a real missile attack, a green outline map of the United States appears on the TV screens at the early-warning stations and at the continental command posts. A series of thin lines, each representing a missile, starts to edge its way toward the American mainland. As the lines draw closer, more lines break away from the original ones, indicating that the individual warheads are streaking toward their targets. At the bottom of the screens, a counter then starts to indicate the number of warheads in the attack.

By simply pressing buttons on their consoles the battle staff in the command posts can call up more precise information. They can observe data on all warheads at once or on individual warheads. The computed impact point of each warhead is given precisely in longitude and latitude and each U.S. target—a city, an airfield, or a command center—is given in code as it is listed in a data bank called the Selected Target for Attack Characterization, or STAC. In a mass attack, the computers will also assess the size of the raid and put it into one of five classes: Class 1, urban-industrial; Class 2, missile fields; Class 3, bomber-tanker bases; Class 4, command and control centers; Class 5, Washington, D.C. This classification would be instantly available to the military commanders and to the president and is the only help the computer will provide in assessing Soviet intentions in an attack. In theory, the president would then select a response from the SIOP.

The immense pressure for immediate action would become overwhelming as the missile counters in the command posts registered the course of the attack, ticking off the numbers of warheads and the seconds before the blasts: "Time of first event," "Time to go," "Number not yet impacted," "Number impacted," "Washington impact time." The flow of information is staggering. The battle staff can call up on their display screens precise details of the launch points of the missiles in the Soviet Union and many of the weapons in the SIOP can be retargeted, almost instantly, if need be. A Minuteman missile with three warheads targeted on Soviet missile silos could be redirected to military command bunkers to avoid hitting empty silos, for example. Once the president or his designated deputy has decided on the response to the computers' assessment of the attack, it is only a matter of pressing more buttons and the computers will oblige with an assessment of actual nuclear damage worldwide. This special system is called NUDETS, for "nuclear detection system." Then, if they have survived, the president and his commanders can choose another option in the SIOP. The computer will do their bidding; it is just as good at attacking as it is at defending.

5

SIOP-62

T HE overkill factor embedded in SAC war plans wor-
ried Dwight Eisenhower so much toward the end of
his presidency that in November 1960 he took the unusual
step of sending his science adviser, Harvard chemistry
professor George Kistiakowsky, to SAC headquarters at
Offutt Air Force Base to review the contingency plans for
bombing the Soviet Union. In particular, Eisenhower
wanted to know how the newly formed Joint Strategic
Target Planning Staff, an uneasy grouping of representatives from all the armed services, was getting along producing the target list for America's first nuclear SIOP. No
one expected the preparations to go smoothly. Since the
end of World War II the bombers of Strategic Air Command had been the main means of delivering America's
growing nuclear arsenal. The air force commanders had
jealously guarded their monopoly and were extremely
reluctant to give any responsibility away. The navy, who
had Polaris submarines that were about to start patrolling
distant waters around the world and who had carrier-

based light bombers, had also fought hard for a place in the center of nuclear war planning. The compromise solution was the formation of a joint targeting staff.

The primary task of the new staff, known by its acronym, JSTPS, was to eliminate duplication of bombing operations. Up to now the air force and the navy had been allowed their own independent targeting, and between 200 and 300 Soviet targets were on the target lists of both services so that, in the event of war, several Soviet cities and ports would have received two nuclear raids, one from SAC's bombers and another from the navy. After many months of bitter wrangling the air force and the navy finally were sitting around a table at Offutt redistributing the Soviet targets. In theory, the result of their deliberations would not only eliminate the duplications, but also reduce the number of weapons required in the war plan. Eisenhower was anxious to see if it could be put into practice. He could have asked his secretary of defense, Tom Gates, to visit Offutt but the president was sufficiently aware of the pressures on Gates from the two competing services to prefer an independent assessment from his civilian science advisor. The president believed that scientists like Kistiakowsky could act as honest brokers between the military and the politicians.

Kistiakowsky was less sanguine about the mission. General LeMay, and his successor at SAC, General Thomas Power, had never developed a reputation for openness, even to military colleagues, about the highly sensitive work at Offutt. A civilian would have even less chance of finding out what was going on, thought Kistiakowsky. He told Eisenhower about his doubts, and the president gave him a special signed order directing SAC to open its books.

Eisenhower also suggested that Kistiakowsky might feel more comfortable about the mission if his technical staff accompanied him, and Kistiakowsky chose George Rathjens from MIT and Herbert (Pete) Scoville, who was assistant director of the CIA and the director of the Office of Scientific Intelligence. Both Rathjens and Scoville had considerable experience in atomic weaponry.

As expected, General Power made the trio feel thoroughly unwanted: He sent a colonel to meet their plane even though, according to protocol, he should have gone himself because Kistiakowsky held cabinet rank. Power quickly made it clear he was prepared to reveal very little. The tour would be limited, he told Kistiakowsky, because there were many things going on at Offutt that were too secret for his civilian ears. He did not want Rathjens or Scoville to take notes of what they saw or heard. The presence of such papers posed too much of a security risk.

Over the next three days, Eisenhower's team spent only one hour being briefed on the details of the SIOP, but they found out enough to be struck by the unnecessary weight of the attacks on Russian cities. Rathjens, trying to make sense of the megatonnage the air force was dispensing, picked a Soviet city of roughly the size and strategic importance of Hiroshima and was shocked to find it was due to be hit with four nuclear weapons, one of which was four megatons with the remaining three of one megaton, each with an explosive power of one million tons of TNT. Hiroshima was destroyed with one bomb, the equivalent of a mere 13,000 tons of TNT.

When the three men returned to Washington, D.C., Kistiakowsky wrote a short memorandum for Eisenhower stressing his concern about the overkill factor. None of the president's original suspicions about the way the targeting was being done were allayed by the report, and Eisenhower confided to his naval aide, Captain Peter Aurand, that the report "frighten[ed] the devil out of me." As a way of reducing SAC's overkill factor, Kistiakowsky suggested that the navy's new Polaris missile force should be held in reserve during the first attack wave and that SAC should be allowed "just one whack—not ten whacks" at each target. The Polaris force could then come in "to clean up what isn't done."

But Eisenhower, who had only one month left in the White House before handing over to Kennedy, took no action on the report. Rathjens was surprised. "I would have thought if the president had reservations about a man in Power's position—and he clearly had reservations —then he would have relieved him," said Rathjens. "Power was a dedicated professional who was determined to do his job and he needed everything he could lay his hands on; never mind the subtleties, the ends justified the means. This may be what is wanted in the Marine Corps, or even at battalion headquarters, but I'm not sure it's what you want at SAC headquarters."

Despite his military background Eisenhower never had a full picture of what was happening at Offutt. He had only outline briefings on SAC's operational nuclear plans, that is, what targets would be hit if he "pressed the button." That is not to say that he was as remote from the planning process as Truman had been; the possibility of a Soviet nuclear attack was sufficiently remote in Truman's day that he could afford not to think about it. But the emerging Soviet nuclear buildup forced Eisenhower to consider such an attack, even though the Soviet arsenal was small and their bombers, still with limited range, would be making a one-way trip.

Throughout his presidency Eisenhower was to struggle with a dilemma about nuclear war that was to confront each successive president more severely than the last: How do you ensure the security of the United States against a Soviet nuclear attack while not appearing to want to fight a nuclear war? A related concern, and another thorny dilemma, was how to deter the U.S.S.R. from attacking Europe, or elsewhere, by threatening a preemptive U.S. nuclear attack that would limit damage to the U.S. to "tolerable levels" while devastating the Soviet Union.

Within six months of Eisenhower's arrival in the White House the Soviet Union tested a 300- to 400-kiloton weapon that they claimed was a hydrogen bomb. It was actually not an H-bomb as such and could not be used in war as it was too big and cumbersome to fit into an aircraft, but clearly it would not be long before the Soviet Union was able to deliver a crippling blow to the U.S. The only question was whether they *might* attack. The new administration was taking no chances: Eisenhower personally believed that the leaders in the Kremlin were not "people who think as we do with regard to human life."

In October 1953, the Administration issued a broader Basic National Security Policy requiring (1) a strong military posture, with emphasis on the capability of inflicting massive retaliatory damage by offensive striking power; (2) U.S. and allied forces in readiness to move rapidly from the start to counter aggression by Soviet bloc forces and to hold vital areas and lines of communication; and (3) a mobilization base, and its protection against crippling war damage, adequate to ensure victory in the event of general war. The Joint Chiefs were so concerned about the prospect of a Soviet H-bomb, however, that they wanted to go further. One JCS study in 1954 suggested "deliberately precipitating war with the U.S.S.R. in the near future" before the Soviet H-bomb had become a "real menace." Eisenhower immediately rejected such an idea and issued an updated Basic National Security Policy stating unequivocally that "the United States and its allies must reject the concept of preventive war or acts intended to provoke war."

At SAC, LeMay took little notice of what was going on in Washington; whatever the politicians were saying about preventive war didn't matter to him because he was concerned with the contingency plans for preventing the delivery of any Soviet nuclear weapons to America. A preventive war might be ruled out by the politicians, but *preemption* was still a strategic alternative. The CIA calculated that the U.S. would have several days', or even weeks', warning of an attack because of the time it would take Soviet forces and bases to prepare themselves. This was the period when the U.S. should strike, thought LeMay, and he believed that "if the U.S. is pushed in a corner far enough we would not hesitate to strike first."

Although Eisenhower repeatedly said he wanted to put limits on SAC's war plans and to curb production of new warheads and especially the size of those warheads, in the end he made no impact on the overkill capacity of the nuclear arsenal. Massive retaliation remained the order of the day. And the guidance, such as it was, from the executive required only that SAC hit their targets with a high level of "damage expectancy." It was up to the SAC commander how to interpret this guidance.

SAC officers continued to produce their own nuclear war plans; so did the navy. With the navy's carrier-based attack planes capable of carrying heavy atomic bombs, the admirals selected, entirely independently of SAC, their own targets in Russia and China. The Joint Chiefs of Staff, recognizing the hopeless muddle the nuclear war plans were in, tried to end the wasteful interservice rivalry for targets, but failed.

The competition over targets generated a demand for more weapons. When the admirals and generals finally agreed to get together in the summer of 1960 to target the U.S. stockpile, it had risen to 18,000 warheads—up from a mere 1,000 five years earlier. In the same period the American list of potential Soviet targets rose from under 3,000 to 20,000. As the U-2 intelligence pictures were analyzed, the SAC targeteers found more installations within the old targets, and this probably accounts for at least part of the sudden increase. If President Eisenhower had ever ordered the U.S. nuclear force into combat, the result would have been a single, massive blow against the Soviet Union, China, and their satellite nations in which more than 400 million people would have lost their lives.

Eisenhower tried, ultimately in vain, to steer the air force war planners away from bombing Soviet cities and to make them concentrate instead on military targets, the so-called counterforce targets. "If we batter cities to pieces by bombing," he asked his JCS in June 1954, "what solution do we have to take control of the situation and handle it so as to achieve the objectives for which we went to war?" In suggesting a "no cities" option in the SIOP, Eisenhower had charted a course that would be followed by his successors over the next two decades and would produce the "rationale" for each new and improved nuclear weapon.

The concept of "massive retaliation" was totally rejected by Kennedy when he took office in January 1961. Together with his defense secretary, Robert MacNamara, Kennedy sought an entirely new strategy that would give the president a SIOP with more than one all-or-nothing option. The new plan would concentrate primarily on counterforce targets, specifically excluding cities from the first attack wave. Reflecting the emerging debate among defense intellectuals for options to the single "Sunday Punch," MacNamara suggested that different plans should be developed for each type of target—a plan to counter the Soviet capacity to deliver atomic weapons, to undermine the main urban-industrial base, or to restrain Soviet aggression in smaller, localized conflicts. The new Kennedy administration would propose such target categories in 1961.

The new plan sounded fine—as though nuclear war could be restricted to a contest between the two opposing forces, as though civilians might somehow escape the horrors, the destruction, and the radiation. But the strategy of "counterforce" did not last long. The air force swiftly seized it as a way of increasing their target list and their stockpile. By the summer of 1967, the American nuclear arsenal had reached an all-time high of 32,000 warheads, including strategic and battlefield weapons.

The classic American postwar dilemma of making the United States a nuclear superpower while at the same time making the world a safe place hit Eisenhower at the beginning of his administration. He had arrived at the White House with a greater understanding of the nuclear stockpile than any president before or since. In 1946, as army chief of staff, he had been the direct link between President Truman and the remnants of the Manhattan Project, which had produced America's first atomic bomb. Like Truman, he was deeply concerned about the failure of international diplomacy to bring about a climate for nuclear disarmament or control. He searched for some kind of hope in his "Atoms for Peace" proposal. He suggested that the weapons powers, then only the U.S. and the Soviet Union, should hand over increasingly greater amounts of fissionable material to an "atomic pool" from which it could then be distributed for peaceful uses. "The amount," said Eisenhower, "could be fixed at a figure which we could handle from our stockpile but which would be difficult for the Soviets to match." The plan was doomed from the start. U.S. intelligence assessments of the production rates of the bombs were abysmally poor. Russia might be producing more, or less. If it were more, equal donations of fissile material to the "atomic pool" would eventually put America at a disadvantage. In the end, the Atoms for Peace program consisted only of an American offer to help other non-nuclear countries start so-called "peaceful" atomic pursuits such as making electricity. In fact, the program succeeded in unlocking the blueprints of nuclear technology for those countries, such as India, who were also interested in making nuclear weapons.

Eisenhower's nuclear dilemma was such that his first step toward nuclear disarmament was quickly overshadowed by two steps in completely the opposite direction. As a military man, Eisenhower had always believed that it was too cumbersome for the military not to have custody of their own nuclear weapons and, within six months of taking office, he transferred to them a sizable number of complete nuclear weapons. No longer was the fissionable material, the uranium and plutonium, kept separately from the bomb casings. The transfers would continue throughout his administration and by 1961 over 90 percent of the stockpile had been transformed into new, completed weapons controlled by the military.

The transfer meant increased readiness for the SAC bomber wings, which Eisenhower specifically excluded from the heavy defense cuts, including other air force reductions in his first budget. In 1953, SAC had a total of 1,500 aircraft including 1,000 nuclear-capable bombers. Eisenhower's budgets projected a quadrupling of the total number of bombers by 1957. For the first time some of these planes would be allocated to Europe for use in a tactical nuclear role. Pentagon reviews suggested that small weapons with yields of 1 to 50 kilotons could be used in battlefield situations in Europe, and the weapons laboratories obliged. By 1954, the engineers were producing a relatively small, by weight, 1,000-pound bomb, the Mark 12, which had the same explosive power as the 10,000-pound blockbusters of earlier years. The new bomb could be carried by almost all of the existing and planned fighter bombers and attack planes. The concept of limited nuclear war was written into official U.S. policy and the planners at Offutt immediately went to work finding "appropriate" targets for the new, smaller weapons.

The mad scramble for targets by the air force and the navy was not a pretty sight. The generals in charge of the so-called nuclear commands—Atlantic, Pacific, and Europe—were determined to defend their traditional right to develop their own war plans with their own targets, and all efforts by the Joint Chiefs of Staff to produce a single, coordinated plan failed. The official air force historians noted with customary restraint that after four years "the defects of the program were clearly more evident than its successes."

The special conferences between the top commanders did nothing to solve the targeting conflicts. The official history records that "duplications and triplications [two or more commands delivering weapons to the same target] were not significantly reduced," but, in fact, 90 percent of the conflicts between the air force and the navy about who would hit a target first were never resolved.

It was left to Eisenhower himself to spell out what he wanted. In his 1958 State of the Union address he said, "A major purpose of military organization is to achieve real unity in the defense establishment in all the principal features of military activity. Of all these, one of the most important to our nation's security is strategic planning and control. This work must be done under unified direction." SAC's General Power, believing that his superior role could continue, supported the president's program and cheekily suggested the creation of a unified U.S. Strategic Command, under the SAC commander of course, to encompass all subordinate units from the air force (heavy and medium bombers and intercontinental ballistic missiles) plus the navy's Polaris fleet and attack planes. The navy protested vigorously, and the top brass bickered for over a year before the generals agreed to a compromise: the creation of the Joint Strategic Target Planning Staff (JSTPS) with the SAC commander as its director and an admiral as his deputy. Even then, the generals argued endlessly over how many representatives there should be from each service. In the end, SAC won. Of 269 seats, SAC had 219, the navy 29, the army 10, the air force (separate from SAC) 8, and the marines 3. Of 34 key positions, those positions in which decisions were made on target selection, SAC and the air force retained 51 percent, a controlling interest.

The stockpile of nuclear bombs took a gigantic leap during Eisenhower's first term. The 1953–54 figure of approximately 1,000 bombs had doubled by the beginning of 1956. An evaluation of how these were to be used is spelled out in a recently declassified 1955 Defense Department document, known as the Weapons Systems Evaluation Group (WSEG), Report No. 12. Although not a war plan as such, WSEG-12 identified a large number of Soviet targets, including 645 airfields and 118 cities. Of the three missions—Bravo, Delta, and Romeo—Delta, the urban-industrial mission, was given the best chance of success, but it was still not expected to bring the Russians to the point of surrender. The Bravo mission, blunting the Soviet's ability to wage atomic warfare, was not rated highly because information on targets was sparse and there were not enough bombs to make it effective; some Soviet bombers were bound to escape the American attack.

The report estimated that the combined atomic offensive would cause a total of 77 million immediate casualties within the Soviet bloc, of which 60 million would be deaths. The majority of the skilled personnel living in 118 Soviet cities would be lost, as would the military and civilian command posts.

Although the degree of overkill was to get much worse than that specified in WSEG-12, the document provides insight into the method of work of the SAC planners. For example, the following is a part of the Bravo section of the report: "In support of the neutralization objective, 645 Soviet Bloc airfields are attacked. Even so, this attack does not encompass all known airfields pertinent to the Soviet operational and dispersal capabilities. Some 320 Soviet emergency airfields remain unstruck. Of this total, about 25 per cent might be temporarily unusable even for dispersal purposes as a result of radioactive fall-out. Thus, during, and immediately after, the U.S. offensive at least 240 unstruck and uncontaminated emergency airfields would be available to the Soviets for the dispersal of their inventory of aircraft capable of delivering atomic weapons. At the beginning of the attack the Soviet inventory is estimated to be approximately 1,530 medium bombers and 3,570 light bombers."

The report underlined the advantage of an American preemptive strike. "The Soviets are estimated to have 284 atomic weapons . . . hence it can be seen that the Soviets need to save only a small fraction of their aircraft inventory and to recuperate only a few of their operating and staging bases in order to be physically capable of undertaking some level of atomic operations *after* [emphasis added] our attack." The fear was that "even under the improbable assumption that only five per cent of the [Soviet] aircraft survived, seventy-five weapons could be lifted against the U.S., and 85 per cent of the remainder of the stockpile could be lifted against U.S. overseas bases and Allies in a single strike as soon as a few bases are recuperated [sic]." The report concluded, "Therefore, if the neutralization offensive is to be made more effective, more weapons must be allocated to this mission to insure coverage of potential dispersal airfields, and to insure that all the important Soviet operational and staging bases are destroyed in the first strike. Further, additional weapons should be allocated for subsequent attacks designed to complete the destruction of the Soviet aircraft inventory, and to prevent the Soviets from recuperating airfields and regrouping and launching their surviving bombers."

On the specific question of the timing of a U.S. attack, the report says that "the Soviets can, in a single strike against the United States, launch more than sufficient one-way sorties to lift all their atomic weapons. Thus, if the Soviets launch such a strike before our offensive is begun, or before our bombs fall on targets, the U.S. offensive may not materially reduce the Soviet atomic capabilities. Therefore, the factor of timing is of vital importance. To achieve a high degree of assurance of destroying all known Soviet operational and staging bases would require an allocation of approximately twice [the number of atomic weapons]. Even this additional allocation cannot prevent the Soviets launching a strike unless we hit first."

Against this background of deep suspicion, and not a little fear, of the Soviet Union's atomic program, it is not surprising that the Joint Chiefs of Staff and the SAC generals were allowed to build up their nuclear forces as quickly as technologically possible. The Joint Chiefs' guidelines certainly did not encourage restraint in the war plans. In the language of the strategic bombardier, they ordered SAC to aim for a 90 percent probability of inflicting *severe* damage to at least 50 percent of industrial floor space in the urban-industrial targets. The order requires translation. An ex-SIOP planner explained, "Severe damage is the highest category—higher than moderate and light. You could look at it this way: Light means rubble, moderate means gravel, and severe means dust." It is easy to see how LeMay justified, to himself at least, allocating several large weapons to a single target. Dust was what the Joint Chiefs wanted. Still at the top of the list were Soviet strategic nuclear targets, and a new category was creeping in—"primary military and government control centers of major importance." Somewhat feebly, the JCS called for an overall plan "which will provide for the optimum integration of committed forces for the attack of a minimum list of targets," but all the time the war plan was getting bigger. By 1956, 2,997 potential targets had been identified; in 1957, 3,261; and by 1960, a staggering 20,000. The huge jump was due, in part, to better intelligence gathering from the U-2 overflights, but it can also be attributed to some wild guesswork about suspected new counterforce, or enemy missile targets.

By the time Kistiakowsky and his two colleagues, Rathjens and Scoville, arrived at Offutt Air Force Base in late November 1960, the JSTPS group had been hard at work for more than three months. Even with their limited access to the files, Rathjens and Scoville discovered how the bombs were allocated. The planners had given each target a point value, with added points for installations of special military significance, such as command posts and atomic bomb factories. Any industry connected with atomic energy scored the highest number of points. The targets and their points were then fed into a computer, and the number of nuclear weapons in the arsenal was allocated according to the number of points. The planners did not always agree with what the computer suggested, however. Moscow, for example, was always a hot favorite to receive more than the computer allowed. "Sometimes they found that too many weapons were going to one target and not enough to another," recalls Rathjens. "Then they sort of eyeballed it."

The result was that every strategic nuclear warhead in the American arsenal, approximately 4,000 at that time, was allocated a primary and an alternate target. The first SIOP, completed in December 1960, revised under Kennedy and eventually known as SIOP-62, required all the warheads to be delivered in one mass attack; there was no delay between the Bravo and Delta targets. This reaffirmation of massive retaliation drew instant, but expected, criticism from the navy. Admirals complained that there had been no effort to assess the minimum force necessary to carry out the objectives of the plan. Furthermore, no nuclear weapons were left in reserve. The overkill factor was, indeed, alarming: SAC had estimated that to comply with the JCS severe damage criteria they would have to assign 300–500 kilotons of weapons to a single target to get the same effect as that achieved by the 13-kiloton bomb dropped on Hiroshima. But, the admirals protested, such massive blasts could produce fallout so serious that it might even affect the operation of nearby friendly forces. One Pacific Command admiral suggested that, if the SIOP were executed, he would have to be "more concerned about residual radiation damage resulting from our own weapons than from the enemy." Eisenhower told his naval aide, Captain Aurand, "We have got to set [target] limits. We've got to get this thing right down to deterrence."

But who was to decide what constituted a "deterrent" to potential Soviet aggression? Not the SAC commander; he wanted as many of the best weapons he could get to threaten the Soviet Union with defeat if they stepped out of line. Not the JCS; they could set guidelines that spoke glibly of "minimum force" but their prime responsibility was to make sure the American military establishment was superior to any of its potential enemies. The JCS were not about to enforce limits when the Soviet Union's ability to respond with a nuclear bomb raid was an unknown, moving target. Over the next two decades the generals would continue to make up the war plan under the theory of "deterrence" by having no second thoughts about a minimum deterrent: The destruction of the enemy, preferably in "one fell swoop," was still the order of the day. Anything less in the atomic age was inviting military defeat.

The politicians looked at deterrence somewhat differ-

ently. As nuclear weapons policymaking now encom-
passed more than a few generals, such as Leslie Groves
and Curtis LeMay, who been the overseers of the birth of
the bomb and the growth of the arsenal, a whole new
breed of civilian nuclear strategists emerged—men and
women who produced a blizzard of papers, analyses, estimates, and forecasts suggesting new and different ways in
which the politicians could interpret deterrence. These
"consultants" showed the politicians how deterrence
could be used to the politicans' advantage. The bomb did
not have to strike terror into the hearts of the American
people; there were ways of "rationalizing" its production,
its storage in the arsenal, and even its use. People would
come to understand that it was the best way of keeping
the Russians at bay. Nuclear deterrence was not a military
plan; it was a political concept, a modus vivendi for the
Cold War, to be used as a political tool. By highlighting a
"gap" in the nuclear deterrent, some nuclear trick or a
gadget the Russians had that the Americans didn't, politicians could show how conscious they were of American
security and how determined they were to maintain it.

The best example of this nuclear opportunism is
Kennedy's spurious "missile gap" of the 1960 presidential
election campaign. Such "gaps" all had the same net result: an escalation of the arms race and a growth in the
SIOP. The civilian nuclear strategists, with their endless
analyses and option papers, played a considerable and
sometimes totally irresponsible part in fueling the arms
race. They always knew more than their attentive audi-
ence, the politicians, and they always knew much more
than the average citizen, who had little access to the nuclear information being fed by the Pentagon into their

"consulting" firms. They were in a position to manipulate the politicians and the public, and they did both for large sums of money. The war fighters, like Curtis LeMay, and the weapons designers, like Edward Teller, continued to play their part, but they were only carrying out orders or pursuing scientific and technological "progress." Ultimately, the strategists—trying to "rationalize" deterrence by constantly seeking new "options" that would somehow limit the amount of damage to the U.S. and somehow make the huge nuclear arsenals more acceptable—were more unseemly and dangerous than the generals or the scientists.

And so the SIOP grew and grew. No politician, from Kennedy to Reagan, has succeeded in paring down the SIOP to the minimum needed to ensure deterrence. When the chance came, in the 1950s and the early 1960s, for Eisenhower and Kennedy to consider a minimum war plan, the so-called "finite deterrence" (a fleet of relatively invulnerable submarines), the politicians allowed the military to bully them out of it. In 1959, the chief of naval operations, Admiral Arleigh Burke, argued that an all-out war was now "obsolete as an instrument of national policy." When the United States had a nuclear monopoly and had been able to disarm the Soviet Union in a first strike, a large land-based force of accurate bombers and missiles had made a lot of sense. But now the Soviet Union had its own missile force, and the U.S. could not hope to destroy all of it in one attack. The U.S. land-based force was itself also vulnerable to attack. The answer, Burke proposed, was a mobile submarine force, which was especially attractive because of its relative invulnerability but also because it lessened the pressure on the politicians to strike first in a crisis. A fleet of 45 submarines, with 29 always on station, would be capable of hitting 464 individual Soviet targets, which would be "sufficient to destroy all of Russia."

Realizing the very real threat posed by Polaris to SAC's monopoly, the air force protested that a single submarine deterrent force would deny the United States a capability to neutralize the Soviet land-based missiles in either a first strike or a retaliatory strike. Polaris was not accurate enough to be used as a counterforce (missile hitting) weapon. To bolster their argument, the air force projected Soviet missile production through the 1960s and, from this projection, indicated that there would be, for the most part 10,400 various counterforce targets, including missile sites and bomber bases, by 1970. To comply with the JCS requirement of a 90 percent assurance of destruction, the air force said they needed 3,000 Minuteman, 150 Atlas, and 110 Titan ICBMs, as well as 900 bombers. How to trim that outrageous demand was the crucial military problem facing John Kennedy when he arrived at the White House in January 1961.

Kennedy flatly rejected the policy of "massive retaliation." As a senator, Kennedy had taken a keen interest in strategic policies and, while he had no instant remedy, he gave the U.S. strategic posture top priority. His secretary of defense, Robert MacNamara, had not been near a military base since serving with the air force during World War II and immediately sought the advice of a small group of nuclear strategists at the Rand Corporation in California. Rand was an air force-sponsored think tank, and throughout the last half of the 1950s the group, including some senior air force officers, conceived a "rational" alternative to "massive retaliation." They suggested a "no cities controlled response" to a Soviet aggressive act, hitting Russian nuclear targets first, and cities only if and when it were necessary. For the first time, a certain portion of the nuclear force would be kept in reserve. The concept had an instant appeal to MacNamara, who liked the idea of having "options" available to the president, particularly options that would leave possible pauses for diplomatic exchanges during the fighting.

MacNamara ordered a revision of the Basic National Security Policy to include counterforce strikes and controlled responses and a new version of the first SIOP appeared in the summer of 1961. It had five options, plus various sub-options. The U.S. attacks were to proceed according to the following plan: (1) Soviet strategic retaliatory forces—missile sites, bomber bases, submarine pens, etc.; (2) Soviet air defenses away from cities, for example, those covering U.S. bomber routes; (3) Soviet air defenses near cities; (4) Soviet command and control centers; and (5) if "necessary," all-out "spasm" attack. By the end of 1961 the United States had an official policy of not targeting Soviet cities. Headlines such as "U.S. War Plan Shift Would Spare Cities" appeared in the American press. Even Moscow was taken off the list of primary targets.

The reaction at SAC was not as extreme as one would have supposed. After recovering from the initial shock of having the White House "interfere" in the war plans literally for the first time, the air force made no great fuss, and it soon appeared that the new strategy could work to the advantage of the targeteers. A National Security Council study, headed by Lieutenant-General Thomas Hickey of

the army, looked at the target lists and the forces required
to carry out a counterforce response and concluded that
a significant growth was needed in both. But Hickey's
calculations of the additional number of weapons needed
was considerably different. The Hickey Minuteman shopping list—150 missiles in 1963 growing to a total of 2,000
by 1971—was a third short of the request made by the air
force. More studies were about to appear that helped the
air force case, however. One of them, a study specifically
on the Minuteman missile system, suggested that all kinds
of improvements in the missile's electronics were needed
to make it capable of replying to "controlled responses."
Eventually these changes cost the Minuteman program
an extra $840 million, or 15 percent of the cost of the
entire 800-missile Minuteman I program. Most important,
both studies suggested that the U.S. land-based missile
force must be made invulnerable or that at least part of
it must be capable of surviving and functioning after a first
strike. This could be done in two ways: hardening the
missile silos in the hope that some of them would withstand the blast of the attack, or making the force larger.
MacNamara chose both, declaring, "We must buy more
than we otherwise would buy." Executive policy was actually providing the impetus for an expansion of nuclear
forces.

MacNamara outlined the new strategy in his now famous commencement address to the University of Michigan at Ann Arbor in June 1962. "The U.S. has come to the
conclusion," he said, "that to the extent feasible, basic
military strategy in a possible general nuclear war should
be approached in much the same way that more conventional military operations have been regarded in the past.

That is to say, principal military objectives, in the event of a nuclear war stemming from a major attack on the Alliance, should be the destruction of the enemy's military forces, not of his civilian population . . . we are giving a possible opponent the strongest imaginable incentive to refrain from striking our own cities." But the new strategy came under fire from two quarters. First, it seemed to many critics that MacNamara was preparing the United States for a first strike against Russia—that, surely, was the result of having a full counterforce capability. There would be no point in shooting your missiles at ones that had already left their silos. A second objection, as Mac-Namara himself would point out, was that sooner or later the Soviet Union would be catching up with the American arsenal so that a full first-strike force was simply unattainable in terms of the sheer numbers of weapons involved. The result was a plan that mixed Soviet urban targets with a second-strike counterforce option. It became known as the "damage-limiting strategy" because it included some effort to "limit" the damage the Soviet Union could do to the United States by hitting the enemy's nuclear weapons.

The air force and navy would still increase their arsenal, however. MacNamara told Congress in 1964, "Such a strategy requires a force considerably larger than would be needed for a limited cities-only strategy . . . it should be large enough to insure the destruction, singly or in combination, of the Soviet Union, Communist China, and the Communist satellites as national societies, under the worst possible circumstances of war outbreak that can reasonably be postulated, and, in addition, to destroy their war-making capability so as to limit, to the extent practicable, damage to this country and our allies." To assure deterrence, MacNamara spoke of the need to be able to destroy 25–33 percent of the Soviet people and 67 percent of their industries. The new strategy buzzword was "assured destruction," which eventually came to be known as the doctrine of Mutual Assured Destruction, or MAD.

MacNamara had been forced to retreat from his efforts to produce a pure counterforce strategy largely because the air force had used the concept to justify huge increases in their missile force, a program that bore no resemblance to a second-strike deterrent. In a memo to Kennedy in 1962 MacNamara wrote, "It has become clear to me that the air force proposals . . . are based on the objective of achieving a first strike capability."

However, the ever-increasing demands on the nuclear force—to hit more targets and be more flexible—were creating serious problems of command, control, and communications, especially with the Polaris fleet. How to keep in touch with a submarine that lived for six months in distant waters without letting your enemy know, through radio and acoustic intercepts, the submarine's location was something completely new to the nuclear planners. By outlining a nuclear war-fighting strategy for the first time, MacNamara had made the general staff think seriously about how to control their weapons systems in the midst of atomic explosions. Other things besides the weapons themselves needed to be upgraded. The JCS had warned MacNamara that the U.S. could not implement his war-fighting (counterforce) policy because the early-warning and command and control systems would not survive an attack. The secretary of defense told

Congress, "We are providing alternate command posts at sea and in the air, with communications links to all elements of our strategic force. With this protected command and control system, our forces can be used in several different ways." A November 1961 study, under U.S. Air Force General Earl Partridge and including outside consultants from the Rand Corporation and the White House, specified what was required. There should be a whole new national command and control system with a main operations room in the Pentagon, an alternate command center buried under a mountain in Pennsylvania (Raven Rock), a command post buried in a mountain in Colorado (Cheyenne Mountain) to receive information from the early-warning stations, and redundant relays to the SAC and Polaris nuclear forces. Finally, this system had to be linked, at all times, with the president; who was, in effect, the headquarters battalion dealing with America's forces. The president and his Joint Chiefs of Staff also needed to communicate with their forces around the world. Efforts to set up a suitable worldwide communications network in support of the SIOP were to prove extremely difficult and hugely expensive.

6

The Wimex

A FEW minutes before midnight on 2 June 1980, five uniformed air force officers of the Strategic Air Command gathered in the entrance to the seven-story headquarters building at Offutt Air Force Base. They signed their names on the duty roster, clipped plastic tags saying "Alert Crew" to their blue cotton shirts, and, clutching brown-paper lunch bags, walked along a corridor lined with photographs of past SAC commanders to an unmarked door. Down four flights they checked in at a desk manned by an armed guard and continued along a gray, concrete-lined tunnel that sloped deeper underground. They passed through two open, solid steel doors and checked in at a second desk also manned by an armed guard. Beside the desk was another unmarked door that was opened when they knocked on it, and the five men disappeared into a darkened room forty-six feet below the ground. They were the officers on the midnight shift in SAC's underground command post, the so-called Delta Team who would spend the next eight hours watching

126

and waiting for any sign that the Soviet Union had started World War III.

Aboveground, SAC's flying command post, a silver Boeing 707 code named Cover All, was sitting at the end of Offutt's runway about to take off. The 21-man crew, each with their own "Alert Crew" tags clipped to their olive-green flying overalls, were about to begin their own eight-hour shift patrolling the skies at 30,000 feet somewhere over midwest America. As they took off another Cover All plane on the 4 P.M. to midnight shift was preparing to land.

Inside the underground post the five officers, with a supporting staff of six enlisted men, took their seats facing a bank of videoscreens and telephone switchboards on the floor of the room, about the size of a football field, with walls twenty-one feet high. The lights are dimmed and mostly there is silence, a hushed, well-cultivated atmosphere that comes of applying professionalism and devotion to their awesome responsibility. The crew faces a wall covered by 16-foot-square screens that display a variety of information about the status of SAC's forces around the world: how many missiles are ready to be launched, how many bombers are ready to be scrambled, whether computers at the early-warning stations are "up" or "down," what the time is in Tokyo or Cape Town or Moscow. In a glassed-in gallery overlooking the alert crew, a dozen empty brown armchairs stand ready for the worst—an emergency that would require the presence of the SAC commander in chief, a four-star general, and his aides.

Such has been the battleground and set routine of the Strategic Air Command's alert crews every day since 3 February 1961, the day of the first flight of an airborne

command post, then code named Looking Glass because
in the air it reflected the mission of the underground
command post. The alert crews are grandly titled "battle
staff," but they have never fought a real battle from their
posts, and they do their jobs each day hoping they never
will. This night, as far as any of them knew, would be
much the same as any other; there would be no battle,
only long, exhausting hours on alert. There was no international crisis on the boil about to push the superpowers
into a nuclear war. America was in the middle of an election year, the Soviet Union was bogged down in Afghani-
stan, and, after Jimmy Carter's aborted attempt to rescue
the hostages in the American embassy in Teheran, that
crisis was stalemated. The crews would not be idle, however. The next eight hours would be punctuated by rigorous routine checks of the early-warning system and of the
alert status of SAC's forces around the world. Periodically,
the crew in the underground bunker would make contact
with the crew in the airplane, just to keep in touch.

Both the battle staff and the SAC commander have permanently open telephone lines to SAC operations worldwide and to the National Command Authority in Washington. On a desk in front of the SAC commander's chair
is a bewildering array of seven telephones, all different
colors. A gold phone links the commander with the Pentagon. In wartime, it is the line that would be used by the
Joint Chiefs to relay commands from the president to SAC
and the rest of his armed forces. In theory, and if time
allowed, the president himself would use it to seek the
advice of his nuclear generals, whose weapons are a part
of the SIOP. The line is not secure, however, because it
travels over the regular, commercial, open lines. If the

commanders want to ensure that their messages will not be understood by outsiders, they use the black phone. This phone encrypts a voice at one end and automatically decodes it at the other, a method that takes a few seconds longer to transmit and to receive. A red phone, marked Primary Alerting System, is the direct link to SAC's missile sites and bomber bases. It carries the initial coded alert order over open lines. To the untutored eye the messages would appear as an unintelligible jumble of letters, but, once decoded, they tell the missile crews to prepare to launch their missiles, and the bomber crews to scramble their B-52s. A gray phone is the command post's normal link to the 352 SAC operations around the world. A blue phone connects SAC to the North American Aerospace Defense Command (NORAD) bunker in Cheyenne Mountain, and a pink phone is plugged into the local telephone company for normal, direct-dial calls. A white phone is the internal Offutt base system.

After exchanging notes with the outgoing shift, the Delta Team senior controller, a full colonel, took the chair in the middle of the line of switchboards and video-screens. Like all men on the alert teams, the colonel was handpicked, his background and work habits approved by the air force's Human Reliability Program. To the colonel's left sat the Warning System Controller, nicknamed the Wisc, whose job is to keep in touch with NORAD and watch two videoscreens, either of which can track the paths of incoming missiles on an outline map of the United States.

Suddenly, without warning, at 2:26 A.M. on the morning of 3 June, the beep alarm on one of the Wisc's screens went off and the screen showed what appeared to be two

Soviet submarine-launched missiles on their way inbound to the United States from the North Atlantic. Swiftly and mechanically the Delta Team went through their emergency action procedures. The Wisc tapped out a command on one of his two computer keyboards calling up a checklist, known as the "decision-matrix," from the computer's memory. The list told him what buttons to push to get more information about the apparent missile threat before calling the Pentagon. The senior controller alerted the SAC bomber crews and put the missile crews on a higher state of readiness. The low warbling tone of an internal alarm broke the silence in the bunker and a red, revolving light flashed eerily around the command post. As the controller pressed the red alert button on his console, he also selected a standard, coded message to be transmitted down the line. The code was "Skybird," ordering the bomber crews to board their planes, start their engines, and stand by for further orders. The major sitting to the right of the controller, known as the Emergency Action Officer, prepared a telex containing confirmation of the controller's Skybird signal. The message was checked for accuracy by another member of the Delta Team in accordance with the strict "two-man" rule governing the execution of any orders having anything to do with nuclear weapons—from guarding them in storage to firing them. The major then read the coded order into the red phone while another crew member listened to check that it was read correctly.

At nineteen bomber bases from Georgia to Maine to California, the Skybird code word created a lot of commotion. Klaxons sounded, and the bomber crews awoke in their special sleeping quarters near the runway, clambered into trucks, and were driven the few hundred yards to their planes. Seventy-six B-52 bombers and an equal number of aerial tankers were scrambled and more than fifteen hundred ground and crew members were alerted. The Skybird signal also scrambled the eight two-man crews of the much smaller FB-111 nuclear bombers on alert, and the 240 missile crewmen in their launch control bunkers.

Next the controller picked up the blue phone to check the missile information on the Wisc's screen with the senior controller at NORAD, 500 miles away in Colorado. If there were an invasion, the NORAD battle staff sitting in front of their videoscreens inside Cheyenne Mountain should be able to confirm it quickly. On a day-to-day basis NORAD tracks anything from missiles to the 4,600 man-made satellites, including pieces of "space junk" from old broken-up space craft to certain physical phenomena, such as sun spots, meteorites, and even moonbeams. Their trick is to weed out the "signatures" made by these natural and known events and distinguish between them from any new or unusual activity. This night in the NORAD command bunker the alert crew had seen something equally alarming. The incoming missile counter on NORAD's main data display was clicking up a series of "2"s like the counter on a pinball machine. Within seconds it showed hundreds of attacking missiles. On another display, a counter ticked seconds away as the "Time to Go" to missile impact was recorded. During one agonizing minute—the time it takes to complete the standard check of the early-warning stations—the NORAD duty officers searched the system for anything that would confirm what they and the Wisc were seeing. But the sensor sites from Alaska to Australia reported no signs of any incoming missiles. As the warning could not be confirmed the SAC controller directed his bomber crews to shut down their engines and await further orders.

Inexplicably, the missiles continued to appear on the Wisc's screen, always in clumps of two's. They also showed up at NORAD, on the computers at the National Military Command Center in the Pentagon and at the alternate national command post inside Raven Rock in southern Pennsylvania. The NORAD radar warning sensors, scanning the distant horizons, still had nothing to report. The duty officer at the Pentagon, the senior Emergency Action Officer, picked up the gold telephone for a conference call on the reported missile attack. By now all three controllers guessed the problem had to be a fault in the computer relay system from NORAD to the other command posts, but, just in case they were wrong, the aircraft combat crews were told to stay in their planes, the missile crews were kept on alert, and, at Pacific Command headquarters in Hawaii, a second airborne command post, code named Blue Eagle, was ordered to take off. The three controllers took precisely one minute to conclude that the missiles on their computer displays were not a threat; clearly the NORAD system had gone berserk. The alert was finally terminated at 2:29:12 A.M. The whole process had lasted three minutes and twelve seconds.

The duty officers voted to end the alert under an established procedure that calls for a majority of them to agree. They took into account three key observations: There was no indication of an attack from the early-warning sensors; the missiles appearing on the screens did not follow any logical pattern of expected attack (if the Russians were invading they would not send their missiles in sets of two's); and the command posts were receiving slightly different information when normally the same information would be received by all the posts. The NORAD controller, accepting that there was a fault in his relay computer, the one that passes the information from the warning sites to SAC and the Pentagon, switched over the whole early-warning operation to a backup system and the phantom missiles faded from the Wisc's screen as suddenly as they had first appeared.

The computer engineers eventually isolated the error in a tiny 46-cent silicon chip that had short-circuited. Within a week the story of the alerts had burst into print with a series of dramatic newspaper headlines, including one declaring, "Nuclear War Was Only One Moment Away." The Pentagon hastened to reassure the world that this was not true, that everything had been under control, and, while the Pentagon was basically correct, the heat of the moment brought vollies of shock and concern from politicians on both sides of the Atlantic. In America, the conservative senator from Texas, John Tower, then the ranking Republican on the Senate Armed Services Committee, said he just didn't believe the Pentagon. In London, the Tory secretary of defence, Francis Pym, coolly told Parliament that there was nothing to worry about; in fact, the news had been more comforting than disturbing because the American early-warning system had proved that it could distinguish between errors or accidents and the real thing.

Pym was right, although it would take a Senate inquiry,

led by the liberal Gary Hart of Colorado and the conservative Barry Goldwater of Arizona, to flush out the details
of what had happened. The inquiry, published in October
1980, concluded, "In no way can it be said that the United
States was close to unleashing nuclear war. . . . In a real
sense the total system worked properly in that even
though the mechanical electronic part produced erroneous information, the human part correctly evaluated it
and prevented any irrevocable action."

But the inquiry also revealed that the June incident was
by no means an isolated one. Other alerts had resulted in
a panic similar to, or even greater than, the one caused by
the dud chip. Three months earlier, in March 1980, a Soviet submarine on a training exercise near the Kurile Islands, north of Japan, had fired four missiles, one of which,
said the Senate report without elaboration, "generated an
unusual threat fan." Another alert occurred on 3 October
1979, when a submarine missile tracking station at Mt.
Hebo, in Oregon, identified the remains of a decaying
rocket dropping from space as an incoming enemy missile. Other, lesser alarms, primarily caused by atmospheric disruptions, totaled 3,703 in the 18 months to the
end of June 1980. All had been routinely and successfully
weeded out of the early-warning system, but air force
officials interviewed by the congressional committee said
that equipment failures, such as the dud chip, caused
alerts two or three times a year. On 9 November 1979, for
example, false indications of a mass missile raid against the
United States were caused by the "inadvertent introduction of simulated data" into the NORAD computer system;
a computer technician had, apparently mistakenly, fed a

training tape, simulating an attack, into the live warning system.

All this put a new gloss on the bland assurances from the Pentagon and politicians like Francis Pym. The Americans had proved they could control the system even if it did go berserk, but other, equally troubling questions remained. The *Congressional Report* observed, "While the controllers at the various command posts were quite effective in recognizing and dealing with erroneous data, could they have dealt with a real attack if it were preceded by stray or erroneous data introduced into the system?" Could the "human factor," faced with the possibility of serious system malfunctions, compile an appropriate list of checks that would really make the system fail-safe?

These were serious questions, but they were somewhat esoteric for most people. To the public, the alerts, as the *Washington Star* put it, had been "a rather scary reminder of the reliance we place on silicon chips and transistors that make up the [military communications] system. How reliable is the system? No one can be sure. America's network of warning sensors, command centers and telecommunications—the so-called Wimex—is complex and sophisticated . . . but the network . . . has been widely criticized for its alleged fragility."

Indeed it had. The Worldwide Military Command and Control System (WWMCCS, or Wimex for short) had a disastrous record. It is the network of computers, warning sensors, command centers, and communications used by the National Command Authorities (the president, the secretary of defense, or their deputies or successors), the chairman of the Joint Chiefs of Staff, and the nuclear regional commands (Pacific, Atlantic, and Europe), plus the "specified commands," such as SAC, to run the military around the world. The early Wimex network was used in a number of international crises requiring immediate response from the command bunkers—the attack on the U.S.S. *Liberty* during the Arab-Israeli war in 1967, the attack on the U.S.S. *Pueblo* in 1968, and the attack on the EC-121 aircraft in 1969—and all of them had revealed a serious flaw in the system: Messages were not relayed fast enough or never reached their destinations. The messages got stuck or delayed in the mass of independent command relay stations.

These incidents had given Wimex a bad name, but congressional inquiries broadened the criticism. They accused the Defense Department of inefficient and ineffective management of its communications and of neglecting training programs and career opportunities for communications officers in order to attract the best and the brightest into the armed forces to help make Wimex work. But the most damning congressional criticism came when the Pentagon finally decided to automate the Wimex in the 1970s and ordered the wrong type of computer. Displaying extraordinary disinterest, the generals ignored warnings from critics, including some on the inside, and wasted millions of dollars patching up a computer system that was simply not designed to do the job it was supposed to do. Several congressional inquiries detailed the stupidity of the purchase and congressmen voiced their alarm at the fact that the Pentagon had failed to provide the nation with a military communications network that would be reliable in time of war, or international crisis. In particular, the new computers were of no use in the execution of the SIOP because they could not process the required amount of information quickly enough.

The limitations of Wimex were painfully discovered during localized, short-lived international crises involving conventional weapons, but the nightmare scenario was always one involving nuclear weapons where a few minutes' delay, the temporary malfunction of a microchip, or the mistaken use of an exercise tape could mean the difference between preventing a nuclear holocaust and being in the middle of one. Yet the military establishment moved incredibly slowly to correct the deficiencies of Wimex. It was not until 1980 that the Pentagon finally overcame past disinterest and neglect. By that time, however, the strategic doctrine had evolved to the point where Wimex was not only required to be reliable enough to *prevent* a nuclear war, but also to fight one. Generals who wouldn't look a computer in the face a decade before went on a fantastic C^3I buying spree.

As the United States expanded its military operations after World War II a system of military communications was needed to connect them all. For many years plans put forward by the Pentagon were resisted by the regional commanders and the four branches of the armed services, who preferred to keep their own, independent networks. But in 1962, after the Cuban missile crisis, President Kennedy, frustrated by his inability to communicate effectively with his forces, personally intervened and ordered the linking of all these disparate commands under the National Military Command System. Wimex was to provide the links. The new system had many initial problems; messages often got lost or were delayed in transit from Washington, D.C., to the forces in the field, and vice versa. In some cases, messages that could have either prevented a crisis or considerably changed the outcome of international events were delayed for absurdly long periods of time because of the bureaucratic and technical deficiencies of the system.

There were three particular examples of how rotten the system was. When the Arab-Israeli war broke out in June 1967 U.S.S. *Liberty,* a 450-foot-long converted World War II cargo ship stuffed with communications gear, was on an espionage mission at the southeastern end of the Mediterranean, a dozen or so miles off the northern coast of the Sinai peninsula and about ninety miles southwest of Tel Aviv. Four messages ordering the ship to move farther away from the coastline were sent from Washington via various commands and headquarters to the *Liberty* on 7 and 8 June. On 8 June, the Israelis maintain they mistook the *Liberty* for an Egyptian ship, torpedoed, rocketed, and napalmed it, killing 34 Americans and wounding 171 on board. The first of the four messages was sent thirteen hours before the ship was attacked, and the last message three and a half hours before, but none of the messages reached the *Liberty* before the first Israeli rockets hit. Two messages were misrouted to the Pacific instead of the Mediterranean. One copy of a message was lost in a relay station and never passed on.

The case of U.S.S. *Pueblo* is no better. Bristling from stem to stern with a topsy-turvy assortment of electronic surveillance apparatus, the ship was wallowing in ground swells off the North Korean port of Wonsan on 23 January 1968 when a North Korean armed flotilla approached. The

North Koreans boarded the ship and captured her crew of seventy-five enlisted men, six officers, and two civilian hydrographers. Two priority messages from the *Pueblo* carrying the flag word PINNACLE (meaning they were to be delivered direct to the National Command Authority) were sent during the encounter. One was delayed by two and a half and the other by one and a half hours en route to Washington. If they had arrived faster, U.S. naval and air support for the *Pueblo* might have arrived sooner— and perhaps even in time to prevent her capture.

The third example is of a U.S. Navy EC-121, a "flying eavesdropper," shot down with a crew of thirty-one by North Koreans while the plane was on a reconnaissance mission over the Sea of Japan early on the morning of 15 April 1969. Prior to the shooting three messages, each reporting that the aircraft was being tracked by North Korean fighters, were dispatched to the Joint Chiefs of Staff from U.S. radar units in South Korea. But the messages were hopelessly delayed. One took three hours, another one hour and sixteen minutes, and the third thirty-eight minutes for transmission to Washington. The third message contained a FLASH flag word requiring it to be transmitted in less than ten minutes.

A 1971 congressional inquiry of these events pointed out that the delays were largely due to people in the communications relay stations not passing the messages on quickly enough, but the testimony also reflected a desperate need to update and automate much of the communications equipment.

No one was more conscious of this need, more determined that it should be done successfully, than David Packard, President Nixon's deputy secretary of defense.

Packard arrived at the Pentagon in January 1969, without any military background, the fourth in a line of Pentagon tycoons, following defense secretaries MacNamara (of Ford Motor Co.); Neil McElroy (of Proctor & Gamble), and Charles Wilson (of General Motors). Packard, an engineer-businessman who had turned a small microelectronics firm in Palo Alto, California, into a multimillion-dollar concern, was, and still is, one of the wealthiest men in America. He had a reputation for being a no-frills, compulsive, shirt-sleeves worker with an unusually modest and easygoing manner. He was not brusque and controversial, like MacNamara, or indecisive, like McElroy, or abrupt and arbitrary, like Wilson. Nixon wanted him to be the Defense Department's manager. A former senator, Melvin Laird, his new secretary of defense, would do the political work.

The six-foot-five-inch Packard received the immediate respect of the generals. "To start with, he's bigger than anyone in the room," said a Pentagon insider, "and he sits there with $300 million stamped on his forehead. Even four-star generals don't talk back." Packard's first assignment at the Pentagon was to direct a review of United States defense policy. He took an instant personal interest in C³I because he found it in total disarray. It became his personal crusade.

The Joint Chiefs had made some rather feeble efforts to offset the problems of Wimex by ordering a whole new set of computers so that the various worldwide commands would be linked by the same "hardware." The JCS had prepared an industry-wide competition to supply the so-called automated data processing (ADP) equipment that they hoped would give Wimex a fast and reliable information-retrieval capacity; any commander hitched into the system would be able to find out instantly all kinds of information about U.S. forces around the world. But Packard discovered no one was really in charge of the project. Without a figurehead the new computer project could not hope to compete effectively with all the other, more visible Pentagon projects for congressional funding. To provide this distinctive leadership, Packard created a new Defense Department Office of assistant secretary for C^3 (the I had not yet been added to the formula), plus a four-man Wimex council consisting of himself, the chairman of the Joint Chiefs, and the two assistant secretaries of defense in charge of intelligence and communications. This group, he hoped, would be able to put its authority behind C^3I programs.

In the next three years Packard also launched a series of projects to make the Wimex command structure more "survivable." He started the flying presidential command posts, Boeing 747 planes converted to "Nightwatch" planes, and expanded the program of converted Boeing 707s, code named "Cover All" planes, for the Strategic Air Command. Packard also accelerated the strategic satellite communications program and convinced Melvin Laird that it was necessary to build simulators to test aircraft communications against the effects of nuclear weapons, especially electromagnetic pulses.

This flurry of activity came to an abrupt halt in December 1971, however, when Packard, citing "strictly personal reasons," resigned. As he left, he warned the nation that the weakest link in America's strategic force was command and control. Asked if the danger was that the nation might not be able to respond to an attack or that the president might not have sufficient flexibility in the war plan, Packard answered, "It's the danger that we might not be able to respond at all . . . I thought this was such an important aspect of the whole nuclear deterrent that we would be irresponsible if we didn't do everything we could [to remedy the situation]."

A few days before he resigned, Packard laid out the future of Wimex in a Defense Department Directive, No. 5100–30. In the cumbersome language of the Pentagon, the order stated, "The WWMCCS serves two functions . . . support of the National Command Authorities is the primary mission . . . support of the Unified and Specified Commands is the second mission. This function [the second one] will be supported by the WWMCCS subordinate to, and on the basis of, non-interference with the primary mission." In other words, the president, the secretary of defense, and the Joint Chiefs had to call on Wimex first at all times. The system, said the order, was to be "the most responsive, reliable and survivable system that can be provided with the resources available." For the first time the U.S. military was to have a fully integrated communications system with a "headquarters battalion" at the top housed in the four command centers—the National Military Command Center (NMCC) in the Pentagon, the alternate center in Raven Rock in Pennsylvania, SAC headquarters at Omaha, and NORAD in the Colorado Rockies. The commander in chief was to be provided with direct links, through the Joint Chiefs, to the operational forces. Should he want to, the president could speak directly to field commanders and, it was hoped, eliminate the disastrous delays experienced in communicating with the U.S.S. *Liberty* and U.S.S. *Pueblo*.

Each of the Wimex command centers, twenty-six in all around the world, would be able to transmit data from one to another through the new automated data-processing (ADP) system, or massive data bank, fitted out with an expensive set of new computers. In theory, each commander would have rapid access to thousands of pieces of critical information, from the number of tanker planes available in Japan to the number of K-rations stored in Korea. Up to now, each of the command centers had developed its own ADP system to suit the needs of the individual commanders. The JCS opened bids for the new system and fierce competition for the contract came from two firms, IBM and the Minneapolis-based Honeywell Corporation, which had just taken over General Electric's computer division. In October 1971, a Defense Department contract for thirty-five computers, worth almost $100 million, was awarded to the Honeywell computer subsidiary, Honeywell Information Systems. It was to become one of the most controversial computer deals ever made.

Even before the deal had been signed, General Seth McKee, the commander in chief of NORAD, bluntly complained to the air force chief of staff that the purchase would "not provide a computer system capable of performing the NORAD mission." But McKee was told, equally bluntly, to stop complaining, that the computers had been bought in a job lot because Honeywell had given the air force a good price and McKee would have to find "some satisfactory resolution for the shortcomings" of the system. McKee's point was that the Honeywell computers would not be able to handle quickly enough all of the early-warning information coming into the command center; in other words, they were not designed to operate, as computer engineers say, in an "on-line real-time environment." They would produce and receive information in so-called sequence processing, or "batches," which tends to create a traffic jam of information in the computer. A Pentagon official would later explain the problem this way: "Suppose the PLO hijacks a plane and lands it somewhere in the desert. I've got to provide help. I need to know where the nearest airfields are, how much fuel they have on hand, how long their runways are, and dozens of other support questions. The computer can't answer and may have to dump, or "batch print-out," a whole set of answers about nearby countries and their airfields—and you have to go through these doggoned things by hand." To convert the computers into types that could operate in an on-line mode would require lengthy and expensive modifications. It was not going to be a cheap buy after all.

The Pentagon's reasoning behind the buy is still a mystery. Repeated requests for access to documents explaining the decision have been turned down. However, investigators from the General Accounting Office (GAO, the congressional audit agency) have, over the last ten years, pieced together a formidable amount of evidence showing that General McKee's original complaint was fully justified. The current NORAD commander, Lieutenant-General James Hartinger, reluctantly admitted in 1981 that the decision to have NORAD buy Honeywell computers was a bad one. "We had to use very complex software to turn those business machines into processing computers in our critical mission area. I think that was a mistake." The forced acquisition of the two Honeywell 6080 computers for NORAD would mean another $60–100 million (depending on whether you take the Pentagon or the GAO figure) to convert them so that they could do the job NORAD wanted. As the new project got under way, the NORAD computer software technicians spent 25 percent of their time trying to fit the computers into the early-warning system. In March 1974, Air Force Systems Command, the overseers of the computer purchase, reviewed the program and concluded that the Honeywell 6080 still needed modification before a real-time, on-line operation could be accomplished. In April 1977, almost one year past the original deadline for bringing the new system into operation, a second air force review group reported that the fully operational capability could not be achieved according to the original specifications. To cope with this unexpected failure, the air force simply lowered their standards; instead of becoming "fully operational," the new system would have "Equivalent Operational Capability," a condition that would be said to exist when the operating capabilities of the new system were essentially the same as the old one it was replacing. In other words, there were no improvements.

One insider, John Huron Bradley, a computer expert hired by the Pentagon to help make the new system work, decided to speak out against the mess the Pentagon had created. Bradley is not everyone's idea of a whistleblower; instead, he fits the image most people have of "Mr. Middle America"—conservative, God-fearing, and patriotic. In the end, it was Bradley's desire to do good that got him into trouble.

Before he joined the Wimex reorganization team in

1972, Bradley, by any standards, had a successful career. After studying electrical engineering and majoring in computers and communications at George Washington University, he wrote two books that became standard texts in the rarefied world of computers. One of them, a detailed technical tract for an IBM computer, sold for $450. In 1970, Bradley started work as a computer consultant to the air force. It was a good job. He lived in a ranch-style home with a swimming pool in a prosperous Maryland suburb. When he moved to the Defense Communications Agency (DCA) to set up the prototype Wimex intercomputer network—the linking of all the Honeywell computers—his job description said he was expected to exercise "a high degree of initiative and self-direction in establishing work goals and in planning and accomplishing his responsibilities." Bradley took this seriously; to him it meant fulfilling David Packard's 1971 directive that the network should be "the most responsive, reliable and survivable system that can be provided." Soon after his arrival at DCA, however, Bradley recognized the key problem with the Honeywell computers—they were not designed to work in an on-line mode. In November 1973, after he had been in that job barely a year, Bradley was ready to tell the Joint Chiefs how difficult it was going to be to hook the computers up and make them reliable, but his superiors did not want to hear. In fact, they wanted Bradley to keep quiet.

One of his project directors wrote a private memorandum about Bradley recommending that he be removed from the project because of "his apparent lack of adaptability and flexibility and his refusal to respond to constructive criticism." Nothing happened to Bradley that time, but six months later, his project director wrote a second letter, again recommending Bradley's removal. In September 1974, Bradley was summarily stripped of his engineering duties and assigned to clerical tasks. Although he protested the transfer under the appropriate government regulation, his protest was rejected. The only consolation was that he kept his engineer's salary. "I was the only clerk in the Department of Defense making $32,000 a year," he said later.

In his new job, working on security—about which he knew nothing—Bradley was not allowed to attend meetings on the Wimex, nor did he see Wimex reports. Nevertheless, he continued to send in his own memos on the reliability issue. The last one he filed was in January 1975. It was ignored, as the others had been.

Over the months, however, other people in the Defense Communications Agency were beginning to have their own misgivings about Wimex reliability. In March 1976 one DCA official reported, "the network crashes [breaks down] approximately every 35 minutes, while the longest time without a crash was approximately one hour." In July 1976 a senior official in the office of the Joint Chiefs wrote, "During recent practice sessions . . . the reliability of system hardware and software was extremely poor. During approximately two weeks of demonstration practices we were unable to complete one full run of the planned demonstration."

In April 1977, Bradley, disillusioned and depressed, yet still determined to be heard on what he considered a grave threat to national security, decided the time had come to bypass his immediate superiors. He took his story to a military aide on the staff of the National Security

Council at the White House. A few weeks later Bradley was summarily fired from his job for "inefficiency, resistance to competent authority and making false and misleading statements about the intercomputer network."

Since his dismissal Bradley has fought a long, tedious battle on two fronts—trying to get his dismissal reversed and trying to win damages from his former supervisors. He has failed on both counts. At 58, the once plump, self-confident professional computer engineer of the early 1970s is a skinny, part-time clerk; the swimming pool in his backyard is covered over now because he can't afford to pay the water bills.

Like many whistleblowers, Bradley paid the ultimate price for his determination to expose the deficiencies of his job and, also as with many whistleblowers, there are undoubtedly two sides to the question still hanging over his dismissal. But it is clear from the evidence presented by congressional inquiries, and particularly by the General Accounting Office, that Bradley had a serious case for the Pentagon to answer. So many reports, official and unofficial, from inside the Pentagon and from outside, have supported Bradley's obsession that Wimex was unreliable. But no one in a responsible position was prepared to take action.

The new computer system was finally switched on at NORAD in September 1979, four years behind schedule, tens of millions of dollars over budget, and only ready to perform a service that the older computers had been offering since 1966. In subsequent congressional hearings on the new system, Representative Jack Brooks, an outspoken Texas Democrat and chairman of the House Committee on Government Operations, commented dryly, "It is not really what you would call riding the wave of the future from the standpoint of computer technology. The technology has moved much faster. We design a program in 1970. In 1975 it is supposed to be finished. It is finished in 1979 with equivalent capability. [Meanwhile] they have picked up a new word. They did not say the thing was ready to go; they said it has equivalent operational capability. They write beautifully out there. You would think they were literary people instead of military."

Tales of military incompetence such as this, cost overruns, completion delays, contract muddles, or worse, have all been well documented. When the subject is a tank, an airplane, a ship, or a missile, politicians and newspapers have found the scandals relatively easy to expose. But it was more difficult to penetrate the dense, intricate problems caused by an unwise computer purchase. The public might never have heard about them but for the false alerts at NORAD and SAC.

Those "glitches" in the system, as the computer technicians call anything that goes temporarily out of order, were soon put right; a separate computer test facility was built at NORAD to avoid further phantom missiles appearing on controllers' screens. In 1981, the Pentagon conceded that the Wimex had all the flaws its critics had been complaining of and exempted NORAD from buying further Honeywell standard computers. And when plans for the latest addition to the national command posts, the Space Defense Operations Center, were completed later the same year, the officers in charge were specifically authorized to find their own computers; the new space mission "far exceeded the capabilities of the current

Wimex standard computers," the Defense Department concluded. Finally, IBM, the loser in the original Wimex computer competition, was asked to build a special system outside Wimex for the most critical element of c^3I: executing the SIOP.

No such quick fixes were available, however, for the rest of the Wimex system still plagued by problems from the purchase of the Honeywell computers. One GAO audit in 1979 concluded that the additional equipment needed to make the computers do what was required had increased the cost of the purchase price by 111 percent. A similar, but larger, growth had occurred at SAC, where costs had risen by 250 percent. Several other reports, from IBM, the Rand Corporation, and the Center for Advanced Computation at the University of Illinois, agreed with the GAO. So did the manufacturers, Honeywell. In a four-page letter to the GAO, Honeywell happily pointed out that it was not their computers that were at fault, but the original design specification from the Department of Defense.

In their own defense the Pentagon maintained that the Wimex was "available" most of the time. But that was not the same as being "reliable" countered the GAO, and reliability was what David Packard had originally asked for, and what the nation should expect of Wimex. That, of course, was also John Bradley's point.

On 6 November 1980, two days after Jimmy Carter lost the presidency to Ronald Reagan, the Pentagon held a command post exercise code named "Proud Spirit." Thirty-five other government agencies took part in a simulated national mobilization in response to a major world crisis. Such exercises are designed to find the weak links—and they did. A major failure of the Wimex left military commanders without essential information about the readiness of their units for twelve hours during the height of the crisis. "Wimex just fell on its ass," was how one of them put it.

What happened, apparently (the detailed results are still locked away in the Pentagon), was that the computer became overloaded and the engineers brought in an interim memory bank called a "buffer" to help relieve the overload, but when they tried to feed the information back into the main system the computer refused it. Even when the computer was working again it behaved erratically. In one case, air force transports were given simulated orders to land at military bases two days before the troops assigned to board them got their marching orders. The computers were also giving the battle commanders more information than they needed. General Edward Meyer, the army's chief of staff, told the Pentagon war planners later, "We must discipline ourselves to only get at the level of data needed to cause decisions to happen." The problem, said General Meyer, was that commanders were "passing too much data back and forth." The army's duty, added Meyer, was "to ensure people are working on the right problems, not the wrong ones."

The right problem was how to make the C^3I system and its central computers work reliably without interfering with the human element of government decision-making. In other words, to have a system that supported the decision-makers rather than controlled them.

Ultimately, the challenge was how to get the generals to focus their attention on buying computing equipment instead of guns, airplanes, ships, and missiles. Wimex was not the best system available at the time it was bought and, by the end of the 1970s, Pentagon computers were on average a full generation behind those in the private sector. This in itself was a scandal, but military computers were not bought to balance ledgers, they were supposed to be reliable enough to prevent World War III. The military had to have not only the best systems, but also systems that could handle the technical realities of controlling nuclear weapons.

7

The Silent Services

ONCE a month a chartered American airliner carrying the 135 crewmen of a nuclear missile submarine
lands at Prestwick Airport on the west coast of Scotland.
The men are transferred by bus to Holy Loch, where a
few days later they board one of the U.S. Navy's thirty-two
"Fleet Ballistic Missile Submarines," or "boomers" as the
submariners call them. The crew spends the next sixty-
eight days about 200 feet underwater in a black-hulled
war machine 560 feet long weighing over 18,000 tons.

Their working day is as unnatural as their environment.
Instead of standard eight-hour shifts, most work six hours
on and six hours off. The only reminder of the normal
twenty-four-hour human cycle is when the boat is "rigged
for red" and a darkroom effect is created as "daytime"
white, fluorescent lights are replaced with red ones. The
most exciting event of the artificial day is eating. Four
meals are served daily, mostly from dehydrated foods,
said to be the best in military dining. But the way to a
submariner's heart is not necessarily through his stomach.

More than 65 percent of submarine officers do not sign on
for second duty tours, and the long periods at sea without
even so much as a letter home mean that only the very
young volunteer.

Given the gravity of the task to be performed, it may
seem surprising that the average age of the boomer crews
is only twenty-four, and, perhaps just as surprising, the
average age of the bomber pilots and missile crews of
Strategic Air Command is only two or three years more.
But in a military system containing 26,000 nuclear warheads, the thousands of young soldiers, sailors, and airmen
with their "fingers on the button" only perform the final
act in the nuclear weapons chain. Their fingers are without authority: They do not make plans, nor do they con-
ceive strategy. They are not trained in the tactical arts of
a fighter pilot, the cunning moves of a tank commander,
or the skirmishing skills of an infantry officer. They do not
even lead men into battle. These are young men in the
first flush of their service careers, when "job satisfaction"
comes from donning a smart uniform and proudly accepting the heavy responsibilities that the armed forces give
much earlier than most civilian jobs. They are prepared
to spend a formative part of their life waiting for a telephone to ring, or a Klaxon to sound, and then furiously
carry out their prepared tasks for the next few minutes in
absolute panic until someone else decides whether the
Soviet Union has started World War III. It is a life of
endless hours of waiting, of incredible boredom.

At the nineteen B-52 bomber bases across the United
States, some 70 six-man crews spend seven days of each
month on alert duty. This means they are always ready to
scramble. They live in part-underground crew rooms at

the end of the runways near their bombers and tanker planes. They can expect at least two full test alerts during the week, and any number of moments of panic due to computer malfunctions or suspect data from the early-warning stations. The missile launch crews, two officers apiece, are on duty for thirty-six hours at a stretch at remote launching centers, mostly in the relentlessly flat, treeless, midwestern farm- and scrublands. They spend twenty-four hours of those thirty-six cooped up in a subterranean capsule forty-one feet long and twenty-six feet wide, crammed in with computers and communications equipment.

The United States military has elaborate regulations to make sure that the critical function performed by these unusual people is never unauthorized. The centerpiece of the regulations is the "two-man rule," which states that working with a nuclear weapon of any kind, anywhere— on a submarine or a bomber, in a silo or a storeroom— requires two people. This means that, at all stages of arming and firing nuclear weapons, the control mechanisms are such that it is physically impossible for one person to perform the task. In addition, there is a host of pre-launch codes and procedures that must be unraveled before the weapons are "armed" and the firing keys will work.

The one leg of the strategic triad of nuclear weapons where this two-man rule is critical is in the missile launch control capsules; these are the only launch platforms for nuclear weapons that actually have only two people. At the beginning of the missile age the launch officers were forty-year-old air force colonels; today, the average age is · twenty-six, mostly lieutenants or captains, and 80 percent of them are in their first air force assignments. Although the launch officers are specially selected and go through searching screenings and assessments of their family background, political and military views, and duty aptitudes, a handful—up to 10 percent—drop out before they ever see a missile command capsule. "I've thought it over and I could never turn the key," is the oft-heard reason. Another 50 percent of them will decide not to stay in the air force past their four-year initial contract period. The launch force turns over once every three years.

This is alarming, but it is only one of the problems confronting the strategic nuclear war planners. They must be sure not only of the execution of the final act of "turning the keys" to fire the missiles, but also that the nuclear forces will work in unison, that only certain weapons will be fired at certain times according to the rigid requirements of the SIOP. In Pentagon language the problem is one of "connectivity," a sort of dustbin term that covers anything from overcoming the difficulties of communicating with submarines in distant waters to being able to turn back bombers already on their way to the target and, finally, to ensuring that young missile officers with small silver keys will do what they are told.

The names of the three generations of U.S. ballistic missile submarines—Polaris, Poseidon, and Trident— have conjured up images of the global reach of the fleet and the omnipotence of the mythical sea gods. The references are well taken. The latest submarine, the Trident, carries twenty-four nuclear missiles suspended under hatch covers in the middle of its big round body. Each of these missiles carries seven or eight warheads with an explosive yield of 100,000 tons of TNT and has a range of

4,000 miles, which means that a Trident submarine can be "on station" north of Newfoundland and, in theory, still hit Moscow. The older Poseidon submarines, which carry sixteen missiles, have more individual warheads than Trident (they average ten per missile), but less range and megatonnage. The Poseidon missile is thirty-two feet long, six feet in diameter, and weighs thirty-four tons. The explosive power of either Trident or Poseidon exceeds that of all the bombs dropped in the last two world wars.

At sea, the missiles are constantly kept in an "up" status, that is, ready to fire at a moment's notice. The missile crews in their blue, lintfree nylon overalls monitor each missile at launch consoles giving information on the missile's temperature, the stability of its guidance system, and the targets its warheads are aimed at. They operate at a high state of readiness. In missile firing drills the Poseidon crews have had fifteen of their sixteen missiles ready for launch 99 percent of the time.

The targets for the missiles are recorded on eight-inch, magnetic disks and fed into the fire control computers. These computers convert the target instructions into trajectories, all the while constantly receiving updated information as the submarine moves through the water, and constantly revising the trajectory of each of the more than 100 warheads. The missile's inertial-guidance system takes it on its arching course, which reaches 700 miles at the highest point, until it is determined to be traveling properly to the target. The rocket engines are then shut down, allowing the missile to glide at almost twenty times the speed of sound to the target on its own momentum.

An order to fire would come in the form of a coded "Emergency Action Message," whose authenticity would be checked by comparing it with an already prepared twin sitting in the submarines' special safe—the "red box." As "main battle stations" are declared by the captain, the sixteen-step sequence of firing the missiles, taking about fifteen minutes, would begin.

Before the missile is launched, the missile tube is pressurized so that it equals the pressure of the water outside. Next, a small rocket in the tail of the missile is ignited. The heat from the rocket boils a pool of water at the bottom of the launch tube and the added pressure from the resulting steam hurls the missile up to the surface, where its main motor ignites, and the missile flies to its target—at most, only thirty minutes away.

The submarines patrol in the Mediterranean, in the northern and western Atlantic and, with the greater range of the Trident, are expanding their operations into the mid-Atlantic and the Pacific oceans. They are literally everywhere: one or two in the North Sea off the coast of Norway, three in the Arctic, some off the coast of Japan and the Aleutian Islands, and a handful in the Kara Sea, the Laptev Sea, and off the Taimyr peninsula—hiding in vast expanses of ocean, yet always within range of the Soviet Union. The pressurized-water nuclear reactor that powers the submarines needs no oxygen, and there is no noxious exhaust. The nuclear reactors will last for several years before they need to be refueled. A desalination plant turns seawater into drinking water, stale air is "scrubbed" to remove the carbon dioxide, and the waste gases are burned in a catalytic converter at high temperatures so that no telltale bubbles are released that might give away the submarine's position. The only technical reason for a nuclear submarine to return to port is food for its crew.

In fact, to avoid detection, the submarines never have to report into base while they are on patrol. This gives the commander a unique degree of autonomy. Although he is supposed to maximize his "time on station," that is, the time spent in any one position within range of the Soviet Union and the submarine's targets, he decides whether his presence in any one particular spot is causing an unnecessary risk of being detected. He can and does receive messages all the time from the Joint Chiefs of Staff and the National Command Authority through a wire antenna trailing hundreds of feet behind the submarine. These messages contain information on the positions of Soviet naval and anti-submarine warfare units, changes in the SIOP, water and weather conditions, changes in his patrol route, new regulations, and promotions. Each member of the crew is allowed four 50-word messages from home during the entire patrol—and sometimes, when the lines are not being used for official messages, they contain an amount of frivolous doggerel that would perplex even the most experienced Soviet eavesdropper. The lines are always kept open, however, both as a hindrance to the Soviets who are trying to make some sense out of the message patterns and as an alarm system known as the "bellringer." If transmissions over the very low frequencies cease, the submarine commander knows he has to take appropriate actions to try to establish communications via other means.

Submarine communications are the most sensitive of all the links with the strategic nuclear forces. The radio oper-

ators have special "Circuit Mayflower" clearances, and
follow strict rules to avoid transmissions that might give
away the submarine's position. A worldwide network of
high-powered communications stations and an airborne
fleet of aircraft known as TACAMO ("Take charge and
move out"), which fly hundreds of miles out over the
oceans for long periods of time, relay the messages from
Washington, D.C., to the submarines. The relayed transmissions via TACAMO, satellites, ships, and land-based stations are said by some to make the submarine vulnerable
to detection, but in over 2,000 submarine patrols since
1960 the Soviet Union has never succeeded in completely
tracking one, according to U.S. intelligence.

When a submarine fires a missile, however, it immediately gives away its position and this presents a grave
problem for the submarine commander. In a mass attack
all the missiles would be fired consecutively, at intervals
of twenty seconds, from forward to aft on one side of the
submarine and from aft to forward on the other side, but
some options of the SIOP call for only some of the missiles
to be fired. The choice could be to hit either 7 targets with
one missile, or 168 targets with all missiles, or any combination in between. As one submarine commander put it,
"If you fire one, you want to fire them all. The tendency
is wanting to save your ass."

Because they run the most invulnerable leg of the nuclear weapons triad, yet also have the most vexing "connectivity" problem, submarine commanders are allowed
to fire their weapons if communications with land-, sea-,
or air-based command posts are cut; they can physically
fire their missiles without the external enabling codes

needed by the land-based forces. The exact procedure for the release of the weapons is secret, but at least four, not two, of the twelve officers on board would have to turn switches—or "vote," as they put it—all at the same time. Four switches must be turned on for the firing circuits to be properly armed and before the missile can be launched. The captain and the weapons control officer have keys for their switches, but the navigations officer must throw a switch and the launch control officer must pull a large lever, called the trigger. To safeguard against wrongful use of the weapons, the launch control officer, the weapons control officer, or the navigator may officially refuse to obey the captain's order to fire, and the alternate launch officers, the executive officer who must verify the captain's commands and the communications officer who must decode the orders, may intervene if they believe that for some reason the proper orders were not received. It is the only case in the whole of the United States armed forces where mutiny is sanctioned.

While the navy controls the survivable submarines containing over half of the U.S. strategic nuclear warheads, Strategic Air Command actually has the bulk of the explosive power with its 2,400 bomber weapons and large number of land missile delivery systems—over 1,000 missiles and 400 bombers compared with 32 submarines. SAC forces are also ahead of the navy in solving their "connectivity" problem.

During most of the 1960s, SAC's strategic bombers were kept on air alert, permanently on patrol with their nuclear weapons, waiting for the call to turn their noses toward the Soviet Union. But in 1968 a B-52 flying over Greenland crashed, spewing plutonium and uranium from its nuclear weapons over the ice-covered ground. Later the same year, a second B-52 collided in mid-air with its refueling tanker and the two planes exploded and crashed into the sea off Palomares, on the coast of Spain. Three nuclear bombs were recovered by U.S. Navy divers. A fourth fell into water over five hundred feet deep and disappeared. The airborne patrols came to an abrupt end and the aging B-52s now never fly with nuclear weapons unless they are scrambled by a genuine alert. Their flying time to the Soviet Union—anywhere between six and nine hours—gives the National Command Authority the unusual luxury in the nuclear war business of being able to recall them and, as such, they are the most controllable of all the nuclear weapons delivery platforms.

Although the main bomber force, the B-52s, has been flying for more than twenty years, the nuclear war planners like heavy bombers because they can deliver a wide variety of nuclear weapons, from small bombs less than the size of the Hiroshima bomb to massive devices weighing four tons and carrying an explosive power of nine million tons of TNT, or seven hundred times larger than the Hiroshima weapon. Most of the B-52s on alert today are armed with four nuclear bombs and four short-range attack missiles, or SRAMs. In the bomber attack scenarios envisaged in the SIOP, the SRAMs would be used to help destroy the Soviet air defenses and the larger bombs would be dropped on remaining missile silos, airfields, dockyards, and other military targets or on urban-industrial centers and Soviet command and control posts.

Today's bomber-delivered nuclear weapons are much more accurate than either the land- or sea-based missiles. The science of dropping bombs from aircraft has progressed enormously since World War II. With the aid of electronic aiming devices they can be dropped precisely on the target, but as one B-52 pilot put it, "It's still like throwing a marble into a paper cup from a moving bicycle."

The bomber's easy recall factor gives the SAC commander, a four-star general, considerable control over them. He can launch his bombers under "positive control"—sending them to a holding position—after receiving an alert from NORAD and before any orders come down from the president. According to the Pentagon, sixty-eight bombers could be in the air in five minutes and a second wave of ninety-five could be airborne within fifteen minutes. If all nineteen U.S. bomber bases were targeted in a Soviet missile attack the Pentagon estimates half of the bomber force would be saved: More than one hundred and fifty bombers would be airborne carrying six hundred bombs and six hundred missiles—half the nuclear explosive power of the U.S. arsenal. From their predetermined holding positions under "positive control," they would then be given their "go code" and turn north to fly over the North Pole to their Soviet targets. The bombers must get through the Soviet air defenses, however, and, despite a vast array of "countermeasures" against radar, attacking missiles, or fighters, they are given only even chances of arriving over the target. That is not the case for the missiles which, once launched, cannot be turned back and carry no self-destruct devices. Most of them would reliably deliver their warheads within less than a mile of the specified target.

The two- or three-acre fenced-off missile control compounds in the American Midwest attract little attention anymore. There's not much to be seen: some flood lights and radar-looking devices, a couple of wooden huts, and a few cars. The sign reads "U.S. Government Property: No Trespassing, Use of Deadly Force Authorized." At the gatepost of the eight-foot chain-link fence is a lone telephone marked "SECURITY." After identification and pass numbers are given over the phone, the electronic gate lock buzzes, loud and clear in the silence of the surrounding scrubland. Inside the small hut armed guards usher the visitor to an elevator leading to the missile control capsule, fifty feet below ground. Another phone and closed-circuit TV identification is used outside the entrance to the capsule for a second security check. Finally, the crew members inside the launch center open the four-ton blast doors that seal them off from the outside.

Leading away from the launch center, like the spokes of a wheel, are buried underground communication links to ten Minuteman missiles. The missiles are deployed three miles from each other in reinforced concrete silos ninety feet deep, able to withstand the blast and pressure of nuclear explosions exceeding twelve times normal atmospheric pressure. Inside the "hardened" silos the missiles are propped up on huge coiled spring "shock absorbers" and the silo itself is covered with a 100-ton concrete hatch. Each of the newest type of missiles in the silos—550 Minuteman IIIs, 60 feet long and weighing 38 tons—has three separate warheads of 170 or 335 kilotons of explosive power, which is almost thirty times the Hiroshima bomb. The older missiles, the 450 Minuteman IIs, have only one warhead with a yield of one million tons of TNT. The huge Titan IIs of the 1950s, now being retired, weigh 165 tons and carry the largest single warhead in the U.S. arsenal— equivalent to nine million tons of TNT.

The two Minuteman launch control officers oversee ten missiles, with five launch control centers in each Strategic Missile Wing. During an alert they strap themselves into red padded chairs, sitting at right angles from each other and separated by the regulation spacing of twelve feet. They each face identical computer consoles that monitor the status of the missiles and would be used to launch them. The missiles are maintained at almost 100 percent readiness at all times and any change in their status is immediately reported to wing headquarters and SAC at Offutt and appears on the SAC command post display screens.

The land-based missiles are the most reliable weapons in the strategic arsenal. Like submarine missiles, but unlike the bombers, they are sure to penetrate the Soviet defenses. Unlike sea-launched missiles, however, the land missiles and bombers have redundant and reliable communications with the National Command Authorities.

Perched on a shelf between the two Minuteman missile crewmen sits the "red box," an exact replica of the red boxes inside the missile submarine command and control center and B-52 cockpits. The red box is secured with two combination locks. Inside are the "validation codes," for authentication of the "nuclear control order," and two keys for missile release. During an attack, an alarm bell inside the capsule rings in response to the initial alert command from the SAC controller at Offutt. The crew then "buttons up"—closes the blast doors and switches to emergency air and power. The senior crew member picks up the red phone, the SAC primary alerting system, and is told by the Strategic Missile Wing command post that an "emergency action message," an authorized launch instruction from the National Command Authority, has been received and will be transmitted over the SAC automated command and control system to the center. An oral twelve number and letter code follows immediately. The crew commander copies it down on a white paper and verifies it with that particular day's launch codes. Simultaneously, a "hard copy" confirmation of the oral message is received over a small teletype machine and each crew member opens one of the two locks on the red box and they remove the sealed "emergency war order" —special instructions for firing the missiles. They also remove their silver firing keys.

The launch officers then jointly "validate" the Emergency Action Message sent over the red telephone. The letters or numbers in the message have to be exact or the crew will not take it as a valid message. The crew then waits for the "release" message, called the "Nuclear Control Order." It can tell the crewmen to launch all their missiles, some of their missiles, or simply to prepare them for launching. The type of order depends on which option of the SIOP the president or his successor has chosen. In some cases the SIOP option may require the missile crew to change the targets of their missiles. Each missile's computers store a choice of targets that can be changed by the crewmen without leaving the launch control center by simply dialing a new set of numbers into the missile's memory. However, the crew never knows what the changes mean in terms of named targets in the Soviet Union.

Before the crews are able to turn their keys to launch their missiles there are two more checks. A second crew, in one of the other four launch control centers attached to their "squadron," must go through the same operations, "voting" positively that the launch command is valid. Also, any one of the crews in the other four capsules can delay, and ultimately prevent, a launch if they believe it is being made as a result of an invalid order. The delay lasts for a few minutes only, after which it is automatically canceled. But the delay mechanism can be reintroduced any number of times, thus ensuring that any crew can be permanently prevented from launching its missiles. In this sense the delay mechanism acts like a congressional filibuster.

Finally, to launch a missile or missiles the two crewmen must turn their keys simultaneously and hold them in position for at least five seconds. During this whole procedure the lit panels on the crewmen's consoles have progressed through several launch sequences beginning with "strategic alert," passing through "warhead armed" to "launch in progress," and ending with "missiles away." Once the missile is fired, there is no recall.

Much has been written about the crazed or errant nuclear weapons' commander, who, acting on his own or as part of a conspiracy, plots to "hot wire" the system and fire off his missiles into the fictionalized world of *Dr. Strangelove* or *Failsafe*. But the hundreds of millions of dollars that have been spent on preventing unauthorized use of nuclear weapons have produced a system that evidently works at the front line—both because of its rigorous list of checks and safeguards and because of the rigid discipline instilled in the young people given the task of actually pulling the trigger.

Far too much attention has been focused on those who turn the keys, who, when asked why they do such a horrible job, often reply that they don't actually think much about it. A more appropriate focus, however, would be the plans and policies that provide the reason for the weapons and their keepers to exist.

8

SIOP-5

THE U.S. Air Force has a nuclear war game called "Big Stick." It's very popular with the young officers who play it at the Air Command and Staff College at Montgomery, Alabama, and one can see why. For five days—the time it takes to complete the computerized game—the players divide themselves into "Red" and "Blue" teams, representing, respectively, the Soviet Union and its allies and America and its allies. The officers become instant commanders of thousands of nuclear weapons, and the purpose of the game is to try and blow each other up. Each team leader issues guidance about strategy, number of weapons, and the types of targets to hit. A supporting staff, some in charge of missiles, some of bombers, some concerned with intelligence collection and so on, create their own model SIOP. When they are ready to play, the two teams sit in front of computer terminals, "sign on" with their own special "passwords," and tell the computer they are ready to do battle. The computer responds with a genial, "Welcome to Big Stick," and off they go.

The game always starts with a conventional war along the border between the Red and the Blue forces, most of the time in Europe. The war escalates rapidly and both sides start using their small nuclear weapons, the so-called tactical nuclear weapons. Once supplies of those weapons are exhausted or nothing is being accomplished with them they can begin to use their "central systems," the strategic weapons. The players select a series of attack plans from their model SIOP, and three separate battles ensue—with bombers, intercontinental land-based missiles, and submarine missiles.

The success or failure of each strike is judged by the Big Stick computer, according to the "Monte Carlo Process," as the air force puts it, which means that playing Big Stick is really like playing a one-armed bandit. Each weapon, a bomb or a missile, has a number known as its Probability of Success factor, or P_s. The teams can work out the P_s factor for each of their weapons from data supplied in the Big Stick handbook. For a land-based missile, for example, the P_s factor might be ninety; that is, 90 percent of the time the missile will be operational—it will launch, find its target, and destroy it. In testing the success or failure of a missile launch on a particular target the computer randomly selects a number and if the number is equal to or less than the weapon's P_s, the mission can be counted as a success; if it is greater than the P_s, the mission is a failure. For example, in the case of the missile with a P_s of ninety, the computer will select a figure larger than ninety only 10 percent of the time.

Each target is allotted a point value, just as they are in

the real-life makeup of the National Strategic Target List for the real SIOP. In Big Stick there are two target lists, one for cities and one for industrial plants. On the Blue side the high-score targets are Washington, D.C., New York, Detroit, and, of course, Omaha. On the Red side they are Moscow, Leningrad, the Baltic port of Riga, and the Soviet naval base of Kaliningrad. A total of forty cities and ninety-four industrial plants carrying the same total number of points are allocated to each side. Although each side has more than enough bombs and missiles to collect the "big points," how successful they are depends on several secondary factors. These include whether the options they chose from their model SIOP turned out to be the most effective and whether they retargeted their missiles correctly as the war progressed.

The winner is the team with the most targets still intact, in other words, the one with the most remaining points. The air force admits, however, that the problem with Big Stick is trying to decide whether the team with the most points can be called a "winner," whether, indeed, there *can* be winners in a nuclear war. "Some would argue," says the Big Stick handbook, "that in any general nuclear war between superpowers both sides will be losers in the real world. Is it reasonable to talk of 'winners' and 'losers' when both sides are destroyed as viable societies? Would a nation consider itself a winner if in destroying its opponent it too was disarmed?"

Computers cannot make such value judgments, of course, so the only requirement for "winning" in Big Stick is meeting the political objectives set out by the team leaders before the game starts. The Big Stick handbook

suggests that the objective should be to prevent the
enemy from "rapidly recovering as a major world power"
and at the same time "ensuring the survival of your own
nation."

But when is this happy state achieved? Is it after one
side has destroyed half of the cities and half of the industrial plants of the other side, or three-quarters, or four-
fifths? The inventors of Big Stick provide no rules here.
The players have to make a case for ending the game to
their team leaders—their "presidents." The handbook
says simply, "You will want to think beyond the concept
of just punishing the other side. This could eliminate
other options for ending the conflict, such as negotiation."
In other words, think of a way of ending the war before
too much is lost.

These young officers can ponder the policy questions
raised by Big Stick, but in the real world the answers come
from politicians, not military men. In 1977, Jimmy Carter
arrived at the White House determined to make significant cuts in the nuclear arsenal. He favored a return to
the lost opportunity of the "minimum deterrent," and
shortly before his inauguration he astounded the Joint
Chiefs of Staff by suggesting that a submarine fleet of two
hundred warheads would be sufficient to deter attack.
Nothing could have seemed more reasonable to Carter, a
one-time submariner with a smattering of knowledge
about nuclear weaponry, but who had not been near the
Pentagon since 1956. The world of the strategic nuclear
deterrent had changed dramatically since those Eisenhower days of massive retaliation—and even since the
days of MacNamara's mutual assured destruction. Richard
Nixon's secretary of defense, James Schlesinger, the first

genuine defense intellectual to fill the top Pentagon position, had introduced the doctrine of "flexible response" and the SIOP Carter saw contained a variety of limited attack options with a hugely increased list of 40,000 potential Soviet targets.

The U.S. military establishment was in the midst of a crucial debate about the need for a new generation of more accurate missiles, a new bomber, and what other measures might be necessary to cope with the Soviet Union's new generation of more accurate missiles. Carter's admirable thoughts of persuading the generals to accept the idea of minimum deterrence that they had rejected twenty years before were soon subsumed by a host of new ideas on how to incorporate new weapons into a new and better national nuclear strategy. A strong team of Democratic defense intellectuals, uncertain of Soviet intentions and flushed with new American technological possibilities, were determined, in some way, to improve on their predecessors in the Nixon administration. Jimmy Carter quickly shed his nuclear innocence. A technocrat, he took a personal interest in the new nuclear machines on the drawing board; he was especially intrigued by the engineering wizardry being dreamed up for hiding and protecting the MX missile. He personally examined the SIOP, prepared new executive guidance for nuclear weapons policy, and, for the first time, required the generals to prepare to fight and "endure" a limited nuclear war.

Instead of a world of smaller arsenals, Carter left Ronald Reagan with all the defense plans and the necessary presidential orders in place to carry out his harder line toward the Soviet Union and more aggressive nuclear stance. Reagan and his lieutenants, who had ironically won election by portraying Carter as weak on defense, set about their appointed task without a smidgen of guile—literally making people go weak in the knees with all their loose talk about "winning" and "prevailing" in limited nuclear wars. The pivotal role Carter played in providing them a springboard was lost in the Reagan rhetoric.

Carter's prodigious interest in nuclear weapons, his desire to put his own stamp on a more "enlightened" nuclear policy, and the high caliber of the defense intellectuals he gathered around him—Harold Brown, Walter Slocombe, William Odom, Jasper Welch, Leon Sloss, Ron Stivers, and, to some extent, Zbigniew Brzezinski—created an executive infrastructure on nuclear matters such as America had never seen. If there had ever been any chance of returning to minimum deterrence, of defusing the Pentagon war planners' natural desire to forge ahead of the Russians, of halting the American military mindset of constant acquisition of the bigger and better mousetrap, this was it. Instead, Carter's well-intentioned team, like so many others before them, was seduced by the old idea that deterrence of the Soviet "threat" still depended on staying ahead of the Russians and being able to threaten computer-game-like destruction of what the Soviets cherished most. No studies were done to argue for President Carter's original hope of reducing the arsenal to two hundred missiles on submarines. The triad of nuclear weapons grew, and the number of SIOP options increased to meet new theories of how to ensure deterrence. There were now too many options to call them "limited," as they had been known in President Nixon's day, so they were called "selected." Carter's people took the old plans and the old strategies, processed and refined them with new "rationales," and brought the two superpowers closer to waging a nuclear war than they had ever been before in the nuclear age.

If you happen to be a politician or a defense intellectual, or anyone who makes a living out of thinking about military problems, the really attractive thing about deterrence is that it lends itself to endless elegant analyses. A military officer may bluntly demand *this* number of weapons to hit *that* number of targets to be sure of deterring a first strike from the enemy; the more sophisticated the demands the more realistic he appears. A politician, on the other hand, or a defense intellectual, can play all kinds of tricks with the basic theory. They can say this kind of weapon or that kind of weapon is needed to meet this kind of threat or that kind of threat and complain that the generals are asking for too little or too much. They can interpret the usefulness of a weapon and the extent of the threat in the way they choose. An unsuspecting public can be easily persuaded of the efficacy of the deterrence theory by being shown "improvements" that make it more credible.

The gap between the rhetoric and the actual war plans has been an enduring characteristic of the SIOP. Robert MacNamara, for example, talked of mutual assured destruction, thus invoking doomsday images of blowing the enemy population off the face of the earth, yet his war plan in the mid-1960s actually called for hitting the enemy's military forces first, cities second. The deception was purposeful. Early proponents like MacNamara of more SIOP options to make deterrence more credible and more rational, even more "humane," quickly realized that the more a politician talked about "counterforce" strikes—hitting the enemy's missiles, not their cities—the more it appeared he lacked the will to blow up large chunks of the enemy's population. The Kremlin might take anything less than a total commitment to hold large populations hostage as a sign of weakness and might be tempted to start a war believing that it would not entail an all-out response. At the same time, the "counterforce" option—aiming at the enemy's missiles—also suggests that such a politician would be more likely to strike first with his nuclear weapons; after all, there is no point in hitting empty missile silos. Worse still, it suggests that such a politician might also believe that hitting only military targets would somehow spare civilian lives.

As the defense intellectuals in the Nixon, Ford, and Carter administrations were suggesting better ways of "ensuring" the credibility of the U.S. deterrent, the Soviet Union was building up its own strategic forces. At the beginning of the 1970s President Nixon's national security advisers, Henry Kissinger and James Schlesinger, both defense scholars who rank among the most formidable American politicians of the atomic age, quickly seized the opportunity presented by the Soviet buildup to put the Nixon administration's stamp on United States nuclear policy. The new controlled response doctrine emerged, designed to give the president more flexibility in the execution of the SIOP. The new doctrine was sold to the public on two levels: as a necessary reply to the Soviet buildup, and as a sensible person's response to the suicide-or-surrender scenarios of yesteryear.

President Nixon himself broached the change in his foreign policy message to Congress in 1970. "Should a president," he asked, "in the event of a nuclear attack, be left with the single option of ordering the mass destruction of enemy civilians in the face of the certainty that it would be followed by the mass slaughter of Americans? Should the concept of assured destruction be narrowly defined and should it be the only measure of our ability to deter the variety of threats we may face? . . . I must not be—and my successors must not be—limited to the indiscriminate mass destruction of enemy civilians as the sole possible response to challenges. This is especially so when that response involves the likelihood of triggering nuclear attacks on our own population. It would be inconsistent with the political meaning of sufficiency to base our force planning solely on some finite, and theoretical, capability to inflict casualties presumed to be unacceptable to the other side." And so, as a first step toward flexible response, we had something called the "doctrine of sufficiency"— yet another interpretation of what might hurt the Soviets enough to deter them.

In 1972, the Defense Department began to study possible revisions of the SIOP to incorporate the new idea. One of the key rationales for creating a new series of limited options was to provide the same nuclear threat to the Soviets on a smaller scale in so-called "theater wars" in, for example, Europe and the Middle East and along the Sino-Soviet border. The United States, said Schlesinger, was still "locked in" to the defense of Western Europe and "our allies have good grounds for asking how we would respond to threats against them from intermediate and variable range nuclear weapons." Any SIOP revision therefore had to contain plans to use both tactical (shorter range) battlefield weapons and strategic (intercontinental) weapons against military targets. There was no guarantee, of course, that the "limited conflicts" would remain limited, but Schlesinger said that he regarded the possibility of a massive attack as "close to zero under existing conditions."

His critics found such certainty that a massive exchange of nuclear weapons was unlikely to follow a limited exchange hard to take; in fact they had difficulty in buying limited options at all. If a limited war seemed likely to turn into a full-scale war, they argued, how was it that limited options, or selected strikes, or whatever they were called, would make massive destruction less likely? Wouldn't the smaller war always end up as a big one?

But the intellectual masters of deterrence had not finished their trick. Up their sleeves were two refinements known as "escalation control" and "damage limitation." Selected strikes, they said, would provide an important breathing space, a pause in the enemy's military activities when diplomacy could go to work. All this depended, of course, on the rationality of the political leaders in the Kremlin, and the question loomed: Was there a limit to the damage a Russian leader would allow to his own country?

Schlesinger told Congress in March 1974, "If we were to maintain continued communications with the Soviet leaders during the war, and if we were to describe precisely and meticulously the limited nature of our actions, including the desire to avoid attacking their urban industrial base . . . in spite of what one says historically in advance that everything must go all out, when the existential circumstances arise, political leaders on both sides will be under powerful pressure to continue to be sensible

. . . those are the circumstances in which I believe that leaders will be rational and prudent. I hope I am not being too optimistic."

The Schlesinger flexible options were eventually codified as National Security Decision Memorandum No. 242, or NSDM-242, and a new SIOP was drawn up known as SIOP-5. While many people accepted, and indeed welcomed, the theory of trying to limit the damage by providing alternative plans to massive retaliation or assured destruction, there remained two lingering doubts: First, how could one be sure of finding Schlesinger's *Homo sensibilis* in the Kremlin? Second, was it not inevitable that the flexible option doctrine would lead to an increase in the arsenal? Clearly, to make more options the planners would be finding more targets, special targets requiring special weapons, not just the old city-busters of yesteryear. Once the weapons laboratories got the word, a host of new designs would appear. Both these concerns initiated long debates that still continue, unresolved.

One remedy was to try and divine Soviet nuclear thought, but as the Soviet arsenal of nuclear weapons became more sophisticated, knowledge of Soviet doctrine concerning their use had actually become less certain. At the best of times, it was hard for Western military strategists to know what Soviet military and political leaders thought about conventional war. Nuclear strategy was even more obscure. Thus, politicians like Schlesinger could devise doctrines for "improving" deterrence based on men making "sensible" decisions, but the war planners in the Strategic Air Command were not impressed by mere reliance on the integrity and rationality of government leaders. As far as they were concerned, there was generic man and there was Soviet man, and they were very different. Moreover, as much as Kremlinologists tried to divine why Soviet man could not be trusted, they tended to interpret Soviet behavior according to their imbedded political biases.

To try and make sense of the confused picture of Soviet nuclear doctrine, the U.S. Air Force did what they had grown accustomed to doing when intellectual problems outfoxed them: They sponsored a study at the Rand Corporation. The study's title, "The Soviet Strategic Culture: Implications for Limited Nuclear Options," reinforced the concept of a vast unknown. However, the author, Jack Snyder, admitted the near impossibility of his task because of the complexity of the problem and the paucity of reliable data. *"No* [emphasis in original] analytical approach to the question of Soviet attitudes toward limited nuclear war can be truly adequate. The age-old lament of nuclear strategists still holds: We have no truly relevant case studies to guide us. Moreover, it seems presumptuous to speculate about Soviet leaders' attitudes toward limited nuclear conflict when those attitudes are doubtless far from fully formed—and, in fact, can never be fully formed until the moment of decision has arrived."

Yet the evolving theory of deterrence required such speculation. There was at least one important difference between American and Russian nuclear strategies that was easy to deduce. Snyder put it this way, "American strategy has been developed in large part by civilian intellectuals and systems analysts . . . Soviet strategy, by contrast, has been developed largely by professional military officers, whose natural inclination, one might suppose, would be oriented more toward military effectiveness than game-theoretical elegance."

Ever since World War II the writings of Soviet military leaders reaching the West had argued that the defeat of the enemy's armed forces was the first and primary objective of military operations in a nuclear war, that nuclear war can and should be "won" in the military sense by destroying the enemy's ability to fight back. (To be fair, the early planners at Strategic Air Command had nothing different in mind. The "Bravo" targets—blunting the enemy's nuclear forces—had been at the top of the list.) The Soviet leadership, working under the confines of a totalitarian state and without an active, free, and open civilian debate, was clearly tied to their military's interpretation in the beginning, but, as the Soviet nuclear capability developed, it also became clear that Soviet nuclear strategy was not monolithic. The Soviet political leadership and the research institutes of the Academy of Sciences, like their counterparts among American political leadership and its attendant defense intellectuals, have also talked of deterrence and proclaimed that there can be no winner in a nuclear war. "Nuclear weapons are held to be blind to the class principle, deterring capitalists and socialists alike," Snyder observed.

Even among the Soviet proponents of fighting a nuclear war, there are some generals who espouse both doctrines of deterrence—a no-win standoff and the need to be able to fight and win a war. They see no fundamental contradiction between the two. Soviet general N. A. Talenskii wrote on the possibilities of strategic surprise and winning nuclear wars in the 1950s, but he has also written about the madness of applying, by another means, the Clausewitz dictum about war being politics to the nuclear age. "In our time," he wrote, "there is no more dangerous an illusion than the idea that thermonuclear war can still serve as an instrument of politics; that it is possible to achieve political aims through the use of nuclear power, and at the same time survive; and that it is possible to find acceptable forms of nuclear war."

Perhaps there was room for maneuver, then; perhaps the Russians would recognize the political declarations of successive administrations wanting to make a name for themselves in nuclear history as just that—rhetoric. But "flexible response" started a second and, in the end, more important debate in nuclear strategy circles about the new doctrine's need for "counterforce" weapons—those that could hit and destroy the enemy's land-based missile force in their hardened silos. Missiles had to be made more accurate. In fact, Schlesinger included a request for research and development funds to improve missile accuracy in his flexible response package and, in two years, tripled funds for nuclear research and development projects in his new counterforce budget.

In the end, flexible response was an excellent example of how politicians and defense intellectuals could declare a policy change in strategic doctrine as though they had only just thought of it when, in fact, for years the military war planners had been doing the same thing in the SIOP. It is worth recalling, for example, that the Emergency War Plans of the 1950s contained three main objectives: Bravo targets, those *blunting* the Soviet ability to deliver an atomic offensive against the United States; Delta targets, those *distrupting* the vital elements of the Soviet war-making capacity; and Romeo targets, those that would *retard* Soviet advances in Western Europe. But the executive branch had never taken enough interest in the war plans to find out what was in them. The Schlesinger doctrine assured that the executive would begin to take a more active part in target selection. Schlesinger's NSDM-242 authorized the secretary of defense to draw up a new document known as the Nuclear Weapons Employment Policy, or NUWEP, setting out the planning assumptions, attack options, targeting objectives, and damage levels needed to satisfy flexible response. The NUWEP also introduced a new option of withholding weapons from certain targets. Some centers of the population—they have never been specified—became "non-targets," completely struck off the list in an effort to make the war plan more "rational." Other targets, such as Soviet command and control centers, leadership headquarters, and the like, were put in a category known as "withholds," those that were to become targets only if diplomatic bargaining broke down during what the planners now called the "intra-war" or "trans-SIOP" period—meaning after the first bombs had dropped. As a final objective in a general nuclear war the NUWEP required U.S. strategic forces to be able to destroy an arbitrary 70 percent of the Soviet industry deemed necessary to achieve postwar economic recovery. At that point the war would be considered "won." However, no defense intellectual or war planner was incautious enough to use the word "win."

When President Carter arrived at the White House in January 1977, he gave the impression, publicly and privately, of being so determined to undo the existing framework of nuclear weapons policy that many believed

NSDM-242 and the Schlesinger NUWEP were destined for the strategic doctrine scrap heap. Far from it. Within three years Carter had prepared five new presidential directives on nuclear war plans—Nos. 18, 41, 53, 58, and 59. Not only did they use the Schlesinger flexible option "counterforce" policy as a starting point, but they actually increased the number and categories of SIOP options and, most important, they required U.S. nuclear forces to be able to endure a nuclear war. The new doctrine was dubbed, grandly, the "countervailing strategy" in an effort to set it apart from the many past efforts at refining nuclear policy in the name of deterrence. The countervailing strategy, said its promoter, Secretary of Defense Harold Brown, would "assure that no potential adversary of the United States or its allies could ever conclude that aggression would be worth the costs that would be incurred. This is true whatever the level of conflict contemplated." Walter Slocombe, the lawyer on the Carter strategic team, spelled it out as though he were preparing a legal contract. "We must have a doctrine and plans for the use of our forces (if they are needed)," he wrote, "that makes clear to the Soviets the hard reality that, by any course leading to nuclear war and in any course a nuclear war might take, they could never gain anything amounting to victory or any plausible definition of victory, or gain an advantage that would outweigh the unacceptable price they would have to pay." The Carter doctrine was billed in the media as a new strategy for nuclear war, but as Brown persistently pointed out, it was only an evolutionary stage in the thirty-five-year development of the U.S. strategic deterrent.

Brown was not trying to mislead anyone. The key presidential directive—No. 59, or PD-59—was only a few pages long, and it did two main things to the Schlesinger SIOP. It shifted some of the emphasis from economic targets onto military targets, particularly Soviet political and leadership targets *and* military command and control targets; it required instead that the U.S. forces be able to "endure" a protracted nuclear war, one that might last perhaps months instead of the few days imagined under the older doctrines that incorporated massive, or "spasm," responses to a Soviet attack. The changes were indeed "evolutionary" variations on a theme, or, as Schlesinger noted lyrically in 1968 about U.S. strategic policy, "Shifting sands seems the best way to characterize the strategic rationales of recent years." The metaphor still applied.

But how did the changes in PD-59 come about? Did they improve deterrence, as the authors claimed? Was the Western world a safer place when PD-59 was translated into the purchase of new weapons and a new SIOP?

A good way of starting to answer these questions is to look at Carter's national security team. Like the Republicans they replaced, the Carter team contained an anti-communist hardliner in Zbigniew Brzezinski as national security adviser and a defense intellectual in Harold Brown, a physicist with many years' experience in nuclear weapons and strategy. Two other team members were important: Walter Slocombe, a young lawyer, an alumnus of the International Institute for Strategic Studies in London, who had started his political life campaigning for George McGovern and later become a Kissinger aide; and William Odom, then an army colonel, a West Pointer, and a Russian linguist who had been a military attaché in Mos-

cow, and was now one of the Pentagon's leading experts
on the Soviet Union and a prominent supporter of war-
fighting plans. President Carter's personal interest in nuclear weapons ensured Schlesinger's NSDM-242, and the
U.S. doctrine of deterrence would undergo a rigorous review by this team. Never before had the war plans had so
much political input.

By the time PD-59 leaked to the press in the summer of
1980, SIOP-5 had been through four regular revisions, each
tagged with a letter starting with A, and each containing
more potential targets and refinements than the one before. The 1980 war plan, SIOP-5D, included a staggering
40,000 potential targets. One might reasonably ask, was
there anything not on the list? Even a country the size of
the Soviet Union does not seem to warrant such attention.
After all, there are fewer than 900 Soviet cities with a
population of more than 25,000; there are fewer than
3,500 key military targets, including 1,398 land-based missiles with 300 launch control centers, 500 airfields capable
of dispatching aircraft and bombers, 1,200 air defense missile sites, 3 submarine bases, 5 naval fleet headquarters,
and about 200 army headquarters. The main Soviet industrial complexes number fewer than 300. That makes a
total of under 4,000 targets.

A hint as to how the gigantic figure of 40,000 is made
up appeared in Defense Department testimony to the
Senate Armed Services Committee in March 1980, the
same time SIOP-5D was enforced. The evidence shows the
extraordinarily comprehensive nature of the targeting
process. First, the targets are divided into four principal
groups. These groups in 1980 contained no urban centers,
per se. They included Soviet nuclear forces, the general-

purpose military forces, Soviet military and political leadership centers, and Soviet economic and industrial bases.
Examples of targets in each principal group were listed by
the Pentagon as follows:

1. Soviet nuclear forces: ICBMs and IRBMs, together
   with their launch facilities (LFs) and launch command centers (LCCs), nuclear weapons storage sites,
   airfields supporting nuclear-capable aircraft, and nuclear missile-firing submarine bases

2. Conventional military forces: caserns, supply depots,
   marshaling points, conventional airfields, ammunition storage facilities, and tank and vehicle storage
   yards

3. Military and political leadership: command posts and
   key communications facilities

4. Economic and industrial targets: (a) war-supporting
   industries, ammunition factories, tank and armored
   personnel carrier factories, petroleum refineries,
   railway yards, and repair facilities; (b) industries that
   contribute to economic recovery—coal, basic steel,
   basic aluminum, cement, and electric power.

Target "sets" from these principal groups are allocated
in four general attack options available to the president:
Major Attack Options (MAOs); Selected Attack Options
(SAOs); Limited Attack Options (LAOs), "designed to permit the selective destruction of fixed enemy military or
industrial targets"; and Regional Nuclear Options (RNOs),
"intended, for example, to destroy the leading elements
of an attacking enemy force." Most important, the SIOP

always left the president with two special attack categories, one for preemptive attacks on the Soviet Union and
another for the so-called Launch on Warning (LOW) or
Launch under Attack (LUA), which mean, respectively, an
all-out retaliation in response to the warning of a nuclear
attack or after an actual attack. There were reserve, or
so-called "withhold," targets, which would not be attacked in any of the four options unless specified. These
include Soviet population centers and national command
and control centers, in theory giving the Soviet leaders an
opportunity to communicate enough with Washington,
D.C., to negotiate an end to the war. In addition, because
the SIOP is a contingency plan for general nuclear war, it
also includes targets in other Communist-controlled
countries. There are, for example, thousands of targets in
the Warsaw Pact nations, in China, in Cuba, and in Viet-
nam, and even some targets in unspecified "allied and
neutral territory."

Such a breakdown makes a little more sense of the
40,000 targets, but where were the weapons to hit the
targets? The United States has about 10,000 warheads in
the strategic nuclear arsenal, so no more than a quarter
of the targets could be hit in the most apocalyptic scenario. And the actual figure for weapons is much less
because in order to assure destruction some of the targets
are due to receive more than one warhead. Moreover,
unless the U.S. forces were "fully generated"—Pentagon
parlance for being on a total war footing—and were not
already attacked, only about half of the 10,000 weapons
would be available for launching. This kind of arithmetic
puts a different complexion on the cavalier assurances of
the politicians and defense intellectuals who argue that

they are improving deterrence by producing more options for the president. Yet the changes ordered by PD-59
were made in the name of deterrence—of keeping the
U.S. nuclear forces sufficiently advanced in weaponry and
in doctrine to preserve credibility.

PD-59 was also a propaganda exercise. At the domestic
political level, it was shamelessly made public in the heat
of the 1980 presidential campaign, and it temporarily de-
flected some of the conservative criticism of Carter's defense posture. At the international political level, it was
primarily designed to exploit potential Soviet fears of U.S.
bellicosity and thereby theoretically to improve deterrence. A White House official, working on the new targeting plans, said in late 1977, "In the past, nuclear targeting
has been done by military planners who have basically
emphasized the efficient destruction of targets. But targeting should not be done in a political vacuum. Some
targets are of greater psychological importance to Moscow than others, and we should begin thinking of how to
use our strategic forces to play on these concerns."

To this end, the Carter team hinted that they were
targeting Soviet food supplies and troops and defenses in
the Far East. This was designed to reinforce Kremlin concerns about the Soviet empire being able to survive a
nuclear war and to cause Soviet leaders increased concern
over a border war with China. PD-59 paid special attention to targets that, if destroyed, would make it hard for
the Kremlin to continue its central control; regional insur-
rection would become a serious possibility during the "in-
tra"- or "post"-war period, announced the Carter team.
National Security Adviser Brzezinski was especially keen
on this refinement. During an early briefing on the new

targeting plans Brzezinski became agitated because the plans did not include attacks specifically on ethnic Russians. Brzezinski, a Pole by birth, complained that the *ethnic Russians* were the enemy, not the other peoples of the Soviet Union, and that there should be options for destroying them.

Finally, PD-59 required the U.S. nuclear forces to be able to endure exchanges of nuclear weapons and maintain a high level of control over a number of different responses and strikes. This was the new part of PD-59, the war-fighting capability. To accomplish this, the presidential directive required two things: upgrading the nuclear forces and upgrading the C³I machinery. The new weapons included the Trident submarine with its more accurate and longer-range missile, the controversial MX in its mobile "racetrack" basing, and the new air-launched cruise missiles. These weapons were required to have targeting packages that could be changed rapidly according to the needs of a war.

The C³I machinery would need more survivability and flexibility. Existing command posts and communications links would be hardened and made mobile. A whole host of new "attack assessment" and "post-strike" reconnaissance and signals intelligence (SIGINT) systems would be required, to increase the ability of the National Command Authority to identify the nature of attacks, choose the most appropriate responses, and gauge their effectiveness.

If the purpose of the Carter administration's release of PD-59 was indeed to appear tough in the midst of the election campaign, it succeeded. There was a lot of loose talk in the media about "new policies" and about "war fighting." But what really mattered, of course, was how the Russians saw it: PD-59's effectiveness depended on the Russians believing that the United States had what military people love to call the *capability* to carry out the directive. The American public might have been taken in by rhetoric, but the Kremlin certainly was not. One Soviet analyst reacting to PD-59 wrote, "No matter how hard the American civilian and military leaders try to frighten the Soviet Union with their well orchestrated strategy of counterforce superiority, the U.S. does not possess this kind of superiority because the majority of the systems on which Directive 59 relies will begin to be deployed only in the second half of the 1980s. . . . Naturally [the U.S.S.R.] will not change its strategy simply because someone in Washington has tried to perpetrate another bluff by publicizing another directive—particularly in view of the fact that U.S. political leaders already have published an excessive amount of various types of strategic doctrines, memoranda and directives." To which kind of remark Brzezinski, using the same Cold War banter, replied, "If the Russians don't like it that's too bad; it's not designed to please them, it's designed to deter them."

What had the Carter team produced? There were three basic themes. Two involved a shift in targeting, reflecting the latest interpretation of what the strategic analysts now thought the Soviets held most dear. Economic and industrial targets were downgraded in favor of military targets and command, control, and communications targets, and political leadership targets were given higher priority. But what did this really mean in terms of changes in the SIOP? Military targets already accounted for more than half of the 40,000 potential targets in the SIOP, compared with only 15,000 industrial and economic targets. Also, U.S. war plans have always included command and control posts and political leadership bunkers; in fact, in SIOP-5D, about 2,000 of the potential 40,000 targets are Soviet leadership targets. Indeed, the number of "leadership" targets had been growing for several years as they had been purposefully sought out and identified by the intelligence collectors. The third theme was something altogether different: It required the U.S. forces to be able to "endure" a nuclear war of "selected" strikes that would in turn justify new weapons and war-fighting devices. Even so, the new doctrine would still be "damage-limiting." That is, PD-59 would prevent the big city populations of the United States and its allies from being blown up because no Soviet cities were being targeted "per se" —therefore the Soviets wouldn't target American or allied cities. *Homo sensibilis* would prevail.

But how was this to happen? The mathematics of the various scenarios of "limited" nuclear war are quite straightforward, as Australian strategic analyst Desmond Ball has pointed out, and they do not support the notion that only a few people would be killed. (Even the authors of PD-59 agreed that millions would die on both sides.)

A comprehensive counterforce attack against the United States would involve strikes against the 1,049 ICBM silos, 4 Fleet Ballistic Missile submarine support bases at Bremerton and Charleston, and 46 SAC bomber and bomber support bases. While the ICBM silos are generally located in relatively unpopulated areas, the submarine bases and many of the bomber bases are quite near major cities. U.S. fatalities from such an attack could range from two to twenty million, with fifteen million perhaps the most reasonable guess.

In a comprehensive U.S. counterforce attack against the Soviet Union, the targets would include nearly 1,400 ICBM silos, 3 submarine bases (at Severomorsk, near Murmansk; Petropavlovsk on the Kamchatka Peninsula; and Vladivostok), 32 major air bases, and perhaps 700 other smaller missile sites, many of them in some of the most densely populated areas of the Soviet Union. Deaths from such an attack are estimated to range from 3.7 million to 27.7 million. Four of the ICBM fields are sufficiently close to Moscow that the capital would receive extensive fallout regardless of wind direction. Attacks on the political leadership would raise the civilian casualties even more, as Secretary Brown himself made clear: "Hardened command posts have been constructed near Moscow and other cities. For the some 100,000 people we define as the Soviet leadership, there are hardened underground shelters near places of work, and at relocation sites outside the cities. The relatively few leadership shelters we have identified would be vulnerable to direct attack."

And, finally, how might the Russians know a U.S. attack was supposed to be limited? Desmond Ball observes, "Given casualties of this magnitude and the particular Soviet difficulty of distinguishing a comprehensive counterforce attack from a more general military plus urban-industrial attack, the notion of limiting a nuclear exchange to supposedly surgical counterforce operations appears rather incredible." What he means is that because the Soviet targets are spread over such a wide geographical area it would be extremely difficult for the Soviet leadership to make an accurate "attack assessment" of a U.S. strike; with command, control, and leadership targets clustered near the cities it would be hard to distinguish between a selective strike and an all-out attack.

So what happened to Carter's original idea of reducing the deterrent to 200 warheads? No one expects politicians to carry out their pre-election promises, of course, or even to be faithful to their most firmly held convictions; there are always compromises. But Carter's change is a radical one; it begs greater explanation. An important part of the explanation can be found, strangely, at the CIA.

During the Nixon and Ford administrations, the hard-line, deeply anti-Soviet Republican politicians in the White House had come to distrust, and disapprove of, the way in which the CIA was preparing what is known as the National Intelligence Estimate, or NIE. This is the agency's assessment of the Soviet Union's current nuclear capability and of its future nuclear force structure. Through the 1960s the nagging question was why the Soviet Union was relentlessly building bigger and bigger missiles if it was not planning to achieve nuclear superiority over the United States and an ability to launch a crippling first strike. The 1969 NIE, while acknowledging the buildup, confidently reported that it was "highly unlikely" the Kremlin was planning either. The Russians had too many other military commitments and the U.S. could always "match and overmatch" anything the Russians could build.

Kissinger and Defense Secretary Melvin Laird sought to downplay this optimistic forecast, first because viscerally they didn't believe the Russians were that genial and, second, for purely practical purposes, it did not suit their submission to Congress to spend lots of money on an anti-

ballistic missile system. In fact, all through the first half of
the 1970s the Republicans in the White House took a
much harder line on the Soviet threat than the CIA, demanding more evidence than the agency was producing
for its moderate forecasts. The scepticism of the White
House politicians was confirmed often enough by an executive branch watchdog group called the President's Foreign Intelligence Advisory Board, PFIAB, pronounced
"piffy-ab." This board was made up of military officers,
ex-Pentagon officials, businessmen, and nuclear weapons
scientists, such as Edward Teller. In 1975, the CIA director,
George Bush, agreed to a PFIAB proposal to have a second
opinion of the CIA's estimates by a group of former military officers and defense intellectuals who became known
as Team B. They included men who had impeccable hard-
line reputations—Paul Nitze, the author of NSC-68, America's key 1950 policy document on the Cold War; two
generals; and two defense intellectuals who had been critical of SALT. The leader of Team B was Harvard professor
Richard Pipes, later to become President Reagan's senior
adviser on Soviet and Eastern European affairs. Pipes
evoked hyperbole in his colleagues; on the American political right he was considered quite brilliant. Others
thought much less of him. President Eisenhower's science
adviser, George Kistiakowsky, a veteran of the White Russian army and also a Harvard man, observed, "I can't
rationalize the man for you—that's not possible."

Team B drew conclusions about the Soviet threat that
were much more somber than the CIA's. They suggested
that the Russians, in their quest for world hegemony,
were determined to achieve nuclear supremacy over the
United States and even to attain the ability to "win" a

nuclear war. Although Team B conclusions were never reflected in any official statements of the day, they created an atmosphere about Russian intentions soon reinforced by some new military assessments about the power and accuracy of new Soviet land-based missiles.

These military assessments suggested, for example, that with new guidance systems on the flagship of the Soviet ICBMs, the SS-18, they were going to be able to knock out the U.S. Minuteman missiles in their silos. A U.S. Defense Department aide, James Wade, coined a new strategic missile buzzword, the "window of vulnerability." The Russians seemed to be building war-fighting weapons, just like the U.S. It was against this background of renewed apprehension about Soviet designs that PD-59 was developed and the whole debate about Soviet strategic doctrine was reopened.

Although it is true to say that Jimmy Carter laid the foundations of Ronald Reagan's even more aggressive policy toward the Soviet Union, the Carter strategic team was always extremely careful never to say they thought nuclear wars were "winnable," and never to say that PD-59 required the U.S. to be able to fight "and win" a nuclear war. Walter Slocombe, countering some of the initial press coverage of PD-59, emphasized that PD-59 "does *not* [Slocombe's emphasis] assume that the United States can 'win' a limited nuclear war, nor does it intend or pretend to enable the U.S. to do so. It *does* [Slocombe's emphasis] seek both to ensure that the United States could prevent the Soviets from being able to win such a war and, most critical, to convince them in advance that they could not win. Few Americans who have studied the problem believe that either side could in any realistic sense 'win' a war in which nuclear weapons were used on a significant scale; but it is also critical—and more demanding—to ensure as best we can that the Soviets do not believe they could win such a war." This showed political savvy as well as the clever semantics of a lawyer's pen, but in the real world of military planning it was meaningless: No one plans to fight a war and lose it, as the guileless war planners that Ronald Reagan brought to Washington in 1981 were quick to point out. They would have no such liberal intellectual qualms; from the beginning they talked about providing the United States with nuclear forces that could fight a nuclear war and "prevail."

9
Who's Minding the Store?

CARRYING a black attaché case, the single tool of his unique trade, U.S. Army Lieutenant-Colonel Jose Muratti was in his usual position in the presidential party, a few steps behind Ronald Reagan, when the shots rang out. A combat veteran, Muratti instinctively threw himself to the pavement. A police officer fell beside him, hit by a bullet in the neck, but Muratti didn't wait to see if the man was alive or dead. He scrambled to his feet, ran toward a waiting presidential limousine, and was bundled into it by a Secret Service agent. The car sped away immediately behind the president's own limousine carrying a wounded Reagan, who had been hit under the arm by a bullet from John Hinckley's .22 pistol. It was 2:25 P.M. on Monday, 30 March 1981.

In the melee, Muratti had never lost his grip on the attaché case, which he now clutched to his chest as the cars raced ten blocks to George Washington University

Hospital. Inside the case were the top secret "Gold Codes," the SIOP options, and the president's decision book. The book contains the president's instructions to authorize the release of nuclear weapons and execute the war plan. Wherever the president goes, even just a mile from the White House to the Washington Hilton to give a speech, the attaché case, nicknamed "The Football," is never far behind.

Muratti was one of three military aides, including a navy commander and a Marine Corps major, on The Football detail. Each day the Gold Codes, a jumble of meaningless letters and numbers, are changed by the National Security Agency. One set is delivered to the White House for The Football, and simultaneously in all nuclear command posts around the world duty officers unwrap their own sealed copies of the same codes. This has been the routine since 1962 when a highly classified National Security Action Memorandum signed by Kennedy created the procedures for presidential release of nuclear weapons. Muratti and his colleagues had rehearsed an emergency such as an assassination attempt many times as they whiled away the long hours of waiting in their extraordinary jobs.

Their orders are to stay with the president at all times, even if he is on a hospital operating table, as Ronald Reagan was about to be. Once a president is incapacitated— under anesthesia, for example—a new chain of command must be set up, but it had never been quite clear exactly how this would happen. Apart from anything else, no one could predict exactly how or where any of these emergencies would occur; the president could collapse after a state dinner in the White House, or die in a plane crash miles

from the Capitol, or be the victim of an assassination attempt almost anywhere. But what made the scenarios still
more difficult to predict was the presence of two conflict-
ing sets of rules governing the line of succession, one
civilian and one military.

According to the 25th Amendment of the Constitution,
passed in 1967, and the Presidential Succession Act of
1947, the line of succession goes from the president to the
vice-president, to the Speaker of the House of Representatives, to the President Pro Tempore of the Senate,
and then to cabinet members in order of seniority. But,
in part, those were old rules for old times; the urgency of
modern presidential politics is to find a successor who
could press the nuclear button if need be, not sign congressional bills and carry out executive duties. The secretary of defense is most familiar with these regulations and
Joint Chiefs of Staff Publication No. 13 provides the procedures for the special line of succession within the National
Command Authority, the official body that would authorize the release of nuclear weapons under normal circumstances. That line of succession goes from the president to
the vice-president, to the secretary of defense and his
deputy, and then to the chairman of the Joint Chiefs of
Staff. Every so often, presidential aides and representatives of the secretary of defense check the JCS procedures
to ensure that they are following current White House
guidance.

Before the end of the day, during which Ronald Reagan
underwent extensive surgery to remove the bullet lodged
in his chest, the confusion inherent in the system was fully
exposed by an extraordinary performance by the secretary of state, Alexander Haig. Clearly a man in a panic, he

made himself look foolish by claiming, wrongly, that he was "in control" at the White House while the president's immediate successor, the vice-president, George Bush, was away in Texas. Unfortunately for Haig, the secretary of defense, Caspar Weinberger, was also at the White House that afternoon and, according to the JCS procedures recently confirmed by Reagan's aides, he naturally felt he had a better claim to be in charge pending Bush's return. No one expected World War III to break out while Reagan was on the operating table, but the unseemly scramble to be "in control" did not encourage confidence in the system. It was especially confusing for Colonel Muratti. If Reagan were deemed unfit to lead the country, he had to get The Football to the president's successor—whoever emerged from the fray.

Within minutes of the shooting special numbers started ringing on the White House telephone switchboard in the basement of the Executive Office Building. This imposing, gray stone, Victorian mansion next to the White House had housed the State Department, Navy Department, and War Department before the Pentagon was built on the west bank of the Potomac. The special telephone numbers are carried by all sixteen of the presidential successors mandated by the 25th Amendment, from the vice-president down to the secretary of education. There are four numbers; two go to the White House and two to Camp David, the president's mountain retreat. Any of the numbers pass through the Central Locator of the White House Communications Agency. When a White House number is called, the operators answer, "White House signals," and the callers give their precise locations. It's a sort of national security roll call.

The president's immediate successor, Vice-President George Bush, was several hundred miles away from Washington at the time of the shooting, flying over Texas in his special air force plane to a speaking engagement in Austin. He was immediately notified by radio of the assassination attempt and his plane turned back to Washington, but it would be at least six hours before he arrived at the White House.

As most Americans spent the hours immediately following the assassination attempt watching the sensational moments of the actual shooting filmed by television crews who had been on the scene, a handful of specially selected White House and Defense Department personnel activated the presidential communications systems, code named "Mystic Star" and "Nationwide." This network put the new "president" in touch with his nuclear forces. It was part of the same system that would be used in the event of a nuclear attack on the United States, a system that, in the words of General William Odom, President Carter's chief military aide, had suffered from "benign neglect" for so many years. The Carter administration dusted off the regulations, directives, and operating manuals to "rig the president up for SIOP execution," as they would put it. It was a thankless task, as General Kelly Burke, air force chief of research and development, told Congress in 1982: "We can buy better computers. We can buy better sensors. We can't buy more time." But the doctrine of nuclear deterrence requires at least that one tries. The White House Communications Agency, through "Mystic Star" and "Nationwide," is the hub of the National Communications System formally set up by a White House Memorandum in August 1963, in the wake of the Cuban missile crisis. Kennedy had been horrified to discover, during the crisis, that messages to his military commanders, even to foreign governments and U.S. embassies, were often delayed for hours, or sometimes remained lost in the system. According to its White House charter, the new communications system was to "be responsive to the Federal Government's needs under all conditions ranging from a normal situation to national emergencies and international crises including nuclear attack."

Two secret sections of the Defense Communications Agency, created at the same time, provide the manpower for the White House hub. The Defense Communications Operations Unit works the communications and emergency power supplies at the White House. The Defense Communications Support Unit, according to its charter, "provides certain specialized classified communications facilities from certain remote locations." One of these is Camp David.

The tasks performed by these secret sections are considered so crucial to national security that the people who work in them must pass a special investigation of their backgrounds known as "Yankee White." According to this standard, they must be "unquestionably loyal to the United States," and their immediate family, "relatives or persons to whom the individual is closely linked by affection or obligation," must be U.S. citizens who are "not subject to physical, mental, or other forms of duress by a foreign power."

The highly motivated and dedicated operators of the White House switchboard are indeed extraordinary people, well known to anyone who has worked in the White

House for being able to locate anyone from a politician, American or foreign, to a film star in a few minutes. According to their job descriptions, they "operate switchboards and radio consoles providing communications to the President . . . memorize names, titles, codenames . . . [and] recognize individuals by voice." The day of the shooting, they failed to locate immediately some members of the cabinet. These officials forgot about their role in the presidential succession ladder and had to be found by a special messenger.

While Bush was flying back to Washington, President Reagan's senior aides called an emergency meeting of the cabinet and the National Security Council. And at the Pentagon the battle staff in the National Military Command Center prepared a bulletin of the world political and military situations to see if there was any possible link between the attempted assassination and any strange or unfamiliar movements of Soviet forces.

It had been a normal day; most of America's forces were on Defense Condition Five, the lowest alert status. There was no unusual strategic warning, and relations with the Soviet Union were, as yet, no worse and no better than they had been during the end of the Carter administration. President Reagan's principal advisors—White House Chief of Staff James Baker and Presidential Counselor Edwin Meese—only weeks before had examined in detail the Carter emergency procedures that had been set up with the Joint Chiefs of Staff for presidential command and had found them to be adequate to assure control, continuity, and what the military insists on calling "connectivity." Baker and Meese had gone to the hospital to be close to the president and made sure good communication links were established between them and the White House Situation Room. "Hey, who's minding the store?" Reagan quipped, as the two aides assured him everything was under control.

In fact, Baker and Meese had already set in motion the secret presidential emergency procedures that immediately transferred "command" to the vice-president. But Alexander Haig's propensity for being in charge, which some excused by saying that it was as much because he used to be a four-star general as it was that he was the senior cabinet officer present, was soon to reveal that the presidential succession was not a simple matter.

When the cabinet meeting was over that day shortly after four o'clock, Haig decided to brief the press, in an effort to reassure the American public and the world that the president did not appear to be dying, that there was apparently no international crisis connected with the incident, and that things were under control—his control, that is.

"Constitutionally, gentlemen," Haig declared, "you have the president, the vice-president, and the secretary of state in that order, and should the president decide he wants to transfer the helm to the vice-president, he will do so. He has not done that. As of now, I am in control here, in the White House, pending the return of the vice-president." As he spoke, Haig was somewhat breathless, and the television cameras caught the little beads of perspiration on his upper lip. He did not convey the impression of a man who was in control of anything, let alone the Western world. Curtis Wilkie, a veteran White House reporter attending Haig's press conference, was heard to remark, "Oh, my God, I've just witnessed my first American coup."

Not only did Haig have the line of succession dead wrong, there was also the question of when the president actually relinquishes control. According to the 25th Amendment to the Constitution, prompted by the Kennedy assassination, the president has to declare himself disabled and must notify Congress in writing. If that is impossible, as it could have been if Reagan had gone into a coma after the shooting, the vice-president and a majority of the cabinet must declare him disabled, also in writing. The 25th Amendment has been used twice before—but then only to appoint vice-presidents, not *presidents*. The first time was after Spiro Agnew was forced to quit his office owing to improprieties, and the second was when President Ford moved into the Oval Office after Nixon's resignation and appointed Nelson Rockefeller as his vice-president.

Whatever prompted Haig's gaffe, Weinberger clearly was in charge of pushing nuclear buttons through the National Command Authority control system. According to Pentagon directives, the NCA is "the channel of communication for execution of the Single Integrated Operational Plan." It goes from the president, the vice-president or the secretary of defense right down through the underground bunkers and to the commander of the SAC Cover All airborne command post. The brigadier-general aboard the Cover All plane is the lowest ranking officer in possession of the nuclear codes. But how and when would the authority be passed on?

Here again there are unknowns. "One of the things I'm not willing to discuss is the employment of nuclear weapons or launch policies," Caspar Weinberger told the press in 1982; "those remain classified and we do not discuss that." Pentagon officials never said anything on the matter at the time of the Reagan shooting. All they have ever been willing to offer is a bland assurance that the system will work. During a Senate hearing in 1980, two years before the shooting, William Perry, the number three man in the Defense Department, fended off inquisitive senators who tried to learn more about the procedures. "In other words," observed Senator Gary Hart, Democrat of Colorado, "whether the president or Washington, D.C., exists, the Soviets are still going to be hit?" "That is correct," Perry responded.

Whether anyone really understands the procedures is not clear. By coincidence, the day after Reagan was shot, General Lew Allen, chief of staff of the air force, was appearing before the Defense Appropriations Subcommittee of the House of Representatives testifying in support of the air force budget. John Murtha, a conservative Democrat from Pennsylvania, asked General Allen who would have made the decision to release nuclear weapons if the Soviets had attacked while the president was under anesthesia, and the questions and answers follow. (The hearings were held in secret so some things are deleted.)

MURTHA: Well, what I am saying is, the authority lies within the president, he didn't relinquish authority, he is under anesthesia, who then can make the decision and would have the appropriate apparatus to make the decision to launch on *warning* [emphasis added]?

ALLEN: Sir, you have exceeded my competence in this subject. I would feel much worse about that except it is obvious that Secretary Haig had that a little garbled too.

MURTHA: But you have got to get word, General, is what I am trying to get at.

ALLEN: For me it is easy. That is [deleted].

BILL CHAPPELL (Democrat, Florida): You just tell them all?

ALLEN: No, sir, it has to be the secretary of defense; the JCS is subordinate to the secretary of defense in these matters. That was quickly established yesterday. I don't know what the secretary of defense was doing in the White House, but I presume he was doing the right thing. We were available to respond to the secretary of defense.

MURTHA: From your standpoint, the secretary of defense had the authority to say to you, launch the missiles, you don't need any codes or anything like that, he has the authority. So in a sense the secretary of defense in a situation like that could release the missiles?

ALLEN: The national policy is that the president has to do that.

MURTHA: He is under anesthesia.

ALLEN: I say you really exceeded my competence because I don't know quite how to answer that.

[The cross-examination of General Allen continued with two other congressmen, Jack Edwards (Republican, Alabama) and Bill Young (Republican, Florida), joining Murtha.]

MURTHA: What I am asking is that the person who has to make the decision is under anesthesia, who makes the decision and, of course the chairman or the general don't know.

EDWARDS: The vice-president has to do it.

ALLEN: My understanding is—this is where Mr. Haig

kind of confused it yesterday, so I don't want to say or sound as though I don't agree with the secretary of state —I think Mr. Edwards is correct. As soon as we had contact with the vice-president that confirmed the fact that the *authority* [emphasis added] was there and that he was in an aircraft with appropriate communications.

EDWARDS: As far as you know, he had the appropriate codes and so forth available to him to make those decisions?

ALLEN: As far as I know, that is correct.

YOUNG: General, in the case that the president would be unable to respond, and the vice-president for some reason was also unable to respond, is there another command authority that would have the right, the jurisdiction and ability to respond, if those first two command figures were unable to function? . . . Well, maybe my question should be a little broader, let's say that no civilian authority for whatever the reason was able to respond, is there a military authority that could function?

ALLEN: Only the president has the authority to make those kinds of decisions and, there, the basic answer is no.

YOUNG: The basic answer is no. What is the real answer?

ALLEN: Well, the real answer is no, unless one chooses to imagine scenarios in which large numbers of nuclear weapons have actually dropped in the United States.

It is just such a question—what happens if deterrence fails—that has driven the growth of emergency procedures and communications and control equipment for the release of nuclear weapons. It has been an evolutionary process. In the Truman and Eisenhower eras, during the days of bombers, massive retaliation, and "spasm" responses of the type Curtis LeMay had in mind, it was fine for the president be hauled out of the Washington danger zone on a special train, as the Army Signals Corps intended to do, or to transfer him to ships based at Norfolk, Virginia, as the navy proposed. The days of intercontinental missiles and controlled responses demanded something else. Jolted into action by the Soviet success with *Sputnik I,* the air force communications experts produced a host of early-warning and command and control devices known as "L-systems." There were continental air defense (416L), traffic control and landing (431L), weather observation (433L), intelligence handling (438L), ballistic missile warning (474L), air communications (480L), and satellite surveillance (496L). All the systems were developed independently of one another and by the end of the 1950s the air force commanders set about trying to link them all together; "capping" was the term they used, and, of course, they gave the result a new name, the National Military Command System.

It is important to understand how alien the concept of a centralized system was to the air force. The bomber wings had always been distinct and apart from the fighter wings and each had always managed their own signals and communications. Now they were all to be under one central command structure, which allowed each to communicate with and be responsive to the National Command Authority, with the president at its head. There were all kinds of reviews, of course. One, known as the Winter Study because it was started in the winter of 1959, had no less than two dozen separate panels and 140 participants from various air force agencies, the electronics industry, and the rapidly emerging breed of civilian technocrats known as military consultants. The full-time director was Gordon Thayer, a vice-president of the American Telephone and Telegraph Company, an appropriate choice since his corporation's communications links would be carrying much of the critical message traffic.

The Winter Study was still going when the Kennedy administration came to power in 1961 and the new defense secretary, Robert MacNamara, introduced the new deterrence concept of "controlled response" to a nuclear attack. MacNamara ordered a second task force under a former NORAD commander, General Earl Partridge, to study the new needs of the command and control system so that it could operate his controlled responses. Like the Winter Study, the Partridge group was made up of service officers and consultants. Both studies had finished their work by the end of 1961 and both had come to the same key conclusion: The current command and control system was vulnerable to missile attack and should be "hardened" and made survivable. That should be done by burying the command posts underground, or making them mobile, in other words, airborne. Such a survivable system would give the president a longer decision time and the ability of a more controlled reaction to an attack—at least that was the implication.

In great haste the Kennedy administration began construction of two such "hardened" command posts, the Alternate National Military Command Center, buried in a mountain in southern Pennsylvania about 70 miles from Washington, and a new home for NORAD, a hollowed-out granite mountain called Cheyenne, in Colorado. Two other "soft" command posts already existed, the National Military Command Center on the third floor of the Pentagon, and Strategic Air Command's underground bunker at Offutt Air Force Base. In a war the president might make his first decisions from a third "soft" command post in the White House Situation Room, a small, windowless, wooden box, twenty by twenty-five feet, in the basement of the West Wing of the White House.

The oldest of the posts is the National Military Command Center, in the Pentagon; it was set up in 1959 during the panic over *Sputnik I* and was then known as the "Joint War Room Annex." It is a peacetime as well as a wartime post with direct communications with all subordinate command centers around the world. Like the other special posts, it has links to the nuclear forces, enabling the commanders to bypass other echelons of command and deliver the "Gold Codes" directly to the missile silos, the bomber crews, or the submarine commanders.

The NMCC's twin brother, the Alternate Military Command Center, in Raven Rock, Pennsylvania, is used only in time of nuclear war and is thus a more secret operation. There have never been any public tours of the post, which is built into Raven Rock in the Catoctin Mountains, a spur of the Appalachians. On the south side, that is, the Washington side, all that can be seen of the post are a few antennae sticking up from the top of the mountain. The access road leads from the small Maryland town of Sabillasville to an unguarded entrance road into the mountain. The only clue as to what might be inside is a sign that reads "U.S. Government Property, No Trespassing" and a warning that photographs are not permitted. A better view is available on the north side, where a chunk of the mountain top is fenced off and the trees shaved. There is a concrete road leading into the mountain. The only sign of life is a car or two parked nearby. Eight miles south of the post is the president's weekend retreat, Camp David. Once a secret camp set up by President Roosevelt, it has become famous as a weekend leisure center for the president and visiting VIPs, and sometimes even for signing international agreements. Named after President Eisenhower's grandson and manned by navy and Marine Corps personnel, the site has two swimming pools, a golf course, an archery range, tennis courts, and a bowling alley, but it also has an underground emergency operations center that can serve as a nuclear war command post. It is linked by a buried cable to the post in Raven Rock.

The other mountain command post, run by NORAD in Colorado, was started in the wake of *Sputnik I* but did not begin operations until 1966. It is much bigger than the post in Raven Rock, covering four and a half acres of excavated granite and, on a normal day, housing 500 people in 15 self-contained steel buildings. The entrance tunnel is 7,000 feet above sea level and stretches 1,400 feet inside. The building complex is cut off from the tunnel by two huge steel blast doors, more than 3 feet thick and weighing more than 25 tons each. They are set in concrete pillars 50 feet apart and can be opened or closed hydraulically in only 30 seconds. Behind the doors, the steel buildings are connected by steel walkways and sit on huge steel springs designed to protect the complex from shock waves. There are 1,319 of these springs, each made from 3-inch-diameter steel rods and weighing 1,000 pounds. The whole arrangement is like a massive innerspring mattress.

It took three years for the construction teams to blast their way into the granite, using a million pounds of explosive and extracting almost 700,000 tons of granite. After the huge caverns had been carved out, the wall of the mountain was secured by driving 110,000 steel bolts, from 6 to 32 feet long, into the granite, thus forming a compressed layer on the new surface. The entire surface was then covered with wire mesh to protect the buildings and people from small chunks of rock that might break away. Electrical power is produced by six diesel engines and a fuel storage reservoir contains enough fuel to keep the complex going for about 30 days. When it was built, the post was considered bombproof. But the accuracy of today's missile warheads means that even this "hardened" facility is now classified as "soft."

The SAC command post at Offutt Air Force Base, only 46 feet below ground, was always considered "soft," and, again in the wake of *Sputnik I,* the air force had all kinds of schemes to make it harder. One of them contemplated digging 5,000 feet down. But all these plans were dropped in 1962 when a solution more compatible with Mac-Namara's controlled response doctrine was found: airborne command posts. The idea was to have a flying command bunker permanently aloft to act as a backup if the ground controls were destroyed. Specifically, the airborne posts were to take over the National Command Authority "during the course and after a nuclear exchange." These planes, first called "Looking Glass" because they reflected aloft what the old underground command posts could do below (and later termed Cover All), became the most critical, survivable links in the command chain and would ensure that the SIOP could be implemented.

Operations of the flying command posts, converted Boeing 707s, began in February 1961, with continuous eight-hour airborne alert shifts. The planes had direct communications with the Joint Chiefs of Staff through the Pentagon command post and SAC bomber and missile bases. After the Cuban missile crisis, more planes were added so that by 1965 there was a total of eight "Looking Glass" planes and a fleet of twenty-three support planes, tankers, and radio relay aircraft.

At least one of these command planes had always been available to the White House, but because of the demands made on the president by the new doctrine of limited nuclear war, the Nixon administration decided that a super flying bunker was needed. In 1972 the air force started a program to convert the larger Boeing 747s to command centers, and three became operational in 1975. Originally nicknamed the "doomsday plane," they are also known as "kneecap," a name derived, in a somewhat contrived manner, from the acronym of its official designation—National Emergency Airborne Command Post. The official code name is Nightwatch and with the aid of refueling tankers the plane can stay airborne for a maximum of 72 hours.

On paper, it looked as though the president would survive and be able to maintain the civilian authority over the nuclear forces vested in him by the original Truman document, National Security Council Memorandum No. 30. But in the few minutes available to him, could the president get from wherever he was—in bed, in the bath, out riding horses, playing golf, or even just walking in the

Rose Garden—to the waiting Nightwatch plane? That question was not seriously examined until Jimmy Carter arrived at the White House in 1977.

General William Odom, military assistant to Zbigniew Brzezinski on the National Security Council, was assigned the job of looking into "crisis management" and, in his words, he "became intimately involved in rigging the president up for SIOP execution." "I was very proud of that effort," Odom would later recall, "because it led to the president becoming personally involved in exercising command and control of the strategic forces. I don't think that has ever been done before. Kennedy may have played around with it a little, but the president's attitude toward command and control, particularly of the strategic forces, has typically been one of benign neglect. But President Carter opened up his decision handbook, he really got into the procedures, ran through the numerous scenarios and became very comfortable with it. He wanted to be able to be awakened at three o'clock in the morning and not be confused, and understand what he was going to have to see, or what he was about to hear, what the voice would sound like on the other end of the line, and that sort of thing. We covered that particular aspect of command and control over a period of about a year, or a year and a half, and we achieved a fair amount."

Jimmy Carter's immersion into the SIOP included a ride in the Nightwatch plane, the presidential airborne command post, the first such ride by a president. The result was great skepticism: Carter was concerned that the plane could not stay in the air forever, that it would not withstand the blast, heat, and electromagnetic effects of a nuclear attack, and that few airports could take the large plane. A couple of weeks after Carter's Nightwatch trip, according to General Robert Rosenberg, also assigned to the National Security Council under Carter, a test was made of the system. "Dr. Brzezinski got on the telephone and called the man you all have heard about who carries the little briefcase with all the codes inside," General Rosenberg recalled, "[and Brzezinski said] 'This is an exercise, I am the President of the United States. We have just got warning that a raid of warheads is en route to the United States. Get me out of here. This is an emergency exercise. We are going to war.'"

The president's personal helicopter squadron, parked at Quantico Marine Corps Base, about thirty miles south of the White House as the crow flies, went into action. In theory it could arrive within a few minutes and whisk the president to Andrews Air Force Base, about twenty miles away, and the waiting Nightwatch plane. Or, it could also fly him to Camp David or Raven Rock. The white-topped Marine Corps helicopters have specially picked crews and are on alert at all times. However, the Brzezinski test was a fiasco, as Rosenberg related: "The helicopter that is supposed to be on alert at all times, to land on the White House lawn and whisk away the National Command Authority, almost got shot down by the Secret Service . . . The sum and substance is that the exercise of trying to evacuate the National Command Authority and set up his communications was a nightmare, just a complete disaster."

Carter was so appalled at the performance that he ordered a study of the presidential evacuation plans. The final report, adopted as Presidential Directive 41, concluded gloomily, "it may not be possible to evacuate those members of the National Command Authority in town at the time to either hardened ground bases or airborne command posts."

If the president manages to board his flying bunker or reach any of his underground shelters outside Washington, D.C., he will have a remarkable series of radio communications available to him. In the air he will be able to contact at least three of the Looking Glass planes because two more would be scrambled as soon as the alarm was raised. Each of these planes is commanded by an SAC general and each has the ability to launch the whole force of 1,000 Minuteman missiles in the event of a total loss of civilian control. The president would also be able to communicate with the submarine missile force through the navy radio relay planes, known as TACAMO. But the important question remains: Can the president get into any of these command posts in the ten or so minutes it would take a ballistic missile launched from a Soviet submarine to land on the White House?

Lee Paschall, retired air force general and former director of the Defense Communications Agency, summed it up this way, "That's a very short [decision] time indeed. Moreover, people don't want to believe news like they have launched, the world is coming to an end, it's time for you to launch in return. President after president has called for options, more options. Each option called for imposes an enormous demand and strain on the command and control system. So how are we to solve decision time problems? How can we make warning [time] completely credible to the president or to his successors? How do we ensure that the successors can communicate, can establish contact with the force commanders to execute the retaliation or the strategic reserve, or continue to negotiate, or whatever? That's a very difficult task."

10

Decapitation

FOR more than ten years Strategic Air Command kept a very strange secret about its Minuteman missile force. Eight of the missiles sitting in silos in central Missouri have no nuclear warheads; in fact, they have no warheads at all. In place of the one-megaton thermonuclear explosives normally carried in the missile's cones are small radio transmitters. These are the robot commanders of nuclear war. If the land-based commanders have lost all means of communicating with the nuclear force, these rockets would be launched by an air force general from his flying command post and their transmitters would send a prerecorded "Emergency Action Message"—either an alert code or the nuclear "go" code—to the bombers, missile crews, and submarines.

Only when the post-Watergate Congress forced so many previously secret military projects out into the open did the program become public—and even then the Pentagon was very coy about it. At first there was only a small hint in the air force's 1980 shopping list to Congress, a

300-page book entitled "Missile Procurement Justification"; on page 189 was listed "Emergency Rocket Communications System, MN-16525C," known as ERCS for short. The description underneath read cryptically, "Due to the aging of the system many electronic parts required for repair are not available and/or difficult or costly to obtain." There was no further clue as to what ERCS consisted of, or when or how it might be used. Moreover, the cost of the new parts was only $18.7 million—certainly not enough to elicit much attention in a total missile package of billions of dollars. A full description of ERCS did not emerge until August 1981, two months before Ronald Reagan announced the biggest single increase in the military budget in United States history, and the largest-ever program for command bunkers and communications links to ensure that American nuclear forces would be able to fight a nuclear war. The robot command rockets were an integral part of that program.

As the full meaning of the nuclear "war-fighting" directives of the Carter administration became clear, the Pentagon put together a host of special and secret programs that would help the forces "endure" a nuclear exchange with the Soviet Union and therefore justify the huge amounts being put into the C^3I empire—now over $30 billion a year, or more than 10 percent of the entire defense budget. Most of these programs were so obscure that it was particularly hard for Reagan to make his political points about the need to spend more money on them without losing his audience in a mass of meaningless Pentagon acronyms and space-age notions. One system was well known, however: the so-called "hot line" between Washington and Moscow, which had been in service since

1963. Using this as an example of one of the communications links that needed upgrading to prevent nuclear war, Reagan referred to it as a "red telephone" line to the Kremlin. The next day several news reports hurried into print happily declaring that the president had made another of his frequent bloopers. The hot line is not, and never has been, a telephone. It is a telex machine opened in 1963 and originally routed two ways, a primary link via cable running from Washington, D.C., through London, Copenhagen, Stockholm, and Helsinki to Moscow, and a second radio circuit via Tangier. Today it operates through two satellites, one American and one Russian; it is checked daily where it is kept in the Pentagon and works fine. It could be "upgraded" if it were moved away from the vulnerable Pentagon building, but then it would only serve one single purpose: to help bring a prolonged nuclear war to an end. Its original purpose was to *prevent* a nuclear war.

The "hot line" and ERCS are both old systems, born in the early 1960s when war planners realized they needed new machinery to meet the new threat from the emerging Soviet intercontinental missile force. The SIOP planners conceived a whole new network of communications links, "bombproof" underground bunkers, and airborne command posts. Two decades later, as Kennedy had done before him, Ronald Reagan came to office on the heels of yet another major shift in American nuclear war strategy, one that stressed fighting rather than mere retaliation. The new strategy required greater flexibility in the weapons themselves and put an even greater demand on the ability of command bunkers and communications links to survive nuclear attacks.

The overriding concern among Reagan's defense advisors was that American nuclear forces could be "decapitated"—that 100 Soviet missiles would be enough to make "surgical" strikes on the command posts and communications links and lop the head off "the scorpion." Even the liberal critics of the Reagan nuclear program had difficulty in arguing against this: The C³I system had been neglected for so long it was not easy to oppose improvements to it. As long as the concept of deterring Soviet military advances was tied to nuclear weapons, it made sense to have the best control system available. U.S. forces would not only be able to retaliate if deterrence failed, but also would be able to prevent accidental nuclear war.

The Reagan budget, containing an additional $22 billion for C³I over five years, went far beyond making the nuclear deterrent credible, however. There were schemes that would only be of use in a prolonged nuclear war, inevitably inviting the scientists and engineers to reach back into their cupboards, dust old ideas off the shelves, and also have new fanciful thoughts of how to make command posts and communications survive under nuclear attack. As though they, too, had discovered something new, generals like the SAC commander, Bennie Davis, rose quickly to meet the challenge declaring, "C³I is my highest priority item. Without survivable command and control you cannot execute your forces [sic]." Actually, one of Davis's more famous predecessors, General Thomas Power, had encountered the same problem in the 1950s and had said it better: "Without communications, all I command is my desk."

It is not putting it too strongly to say that C³I has become a fad at the Pentagon. At a time when several visible weapons systems are coming under attack on Capitol Hill, such as the B-1 bomber and the MX missile, funding for C³I passes without any adverse comment. Encouraged by this, the Reagan administration has asked for still more money—$26 billion in 1982 and $31 billion in 1983. C³I is rapidly becoming an entirely new part of the nuclear arms race. Such runaway spending made the defense intellectuals who encouraged C³I more cautious; they warned that money might not be able to solve all the problems. "To develop and deploy all these C³I technologies will be a formidable undertaking," said Charles Zraket, vice-president of the Mitre Corporation, the air force's C³I think tank. "It will cost tens of billions of dollars over the next ten years, above and beyond what we are spending today . . . and it is not clear how long such a system would endure. That would depend on the scope and timing of the attack." Ironically, the most damning comment came from the nation's top soldier himself, General David Jones, chairman of the Joint Chiefs of Staff. On retiring in June 1982, he warned that it would be throwing money into a "bottomless pit" to try and prepare the United States for a long nuclear war with the Soviet Union. "I don't see much chance of nuclear war being limited or protracted," said Jones flatly.

But the ultimate result of all this concentration on C³I could be something of much greater concern: an erosion of the accepted control over nuclear weapons. These technical improvements cannot, in any way, change the amount of time available to the president or to his successors to decide the appropriate response to an attack. That time is now as little as seven minutes if one assumes the attack is from a Soviet submarine in the Atlantic. These new C³I systems continue to ensure that civilian authority is still able to launch a retaliatory attack with a "spasm" decision, but, if the civilian authority is destroyed, the new system also ensures that the military is able to carry on to *fight* a nuclear war—on its own.

The C³I empire has three distinct parts—the early-warning sensors, the command posts, and communications. Without the third part, the first two are useless. An early-warning radar may detect correctly an incoming attack of missiles, but unless that information can be relayed to the command posts, no order can be generated by the commander. By the same token, if the lines of communication are dead between the command posts and the missile silos or the bomber bases, the order will never be received. In strategic nuclear communications that order is the short, coded, presidential Emergency Action Message, or EAM, which tells the forces when to attack, when to hold fire, and when to cease fire. Several different types of communications lines are open to the "war fighters"—normal telephone lines, linked by land and sea cables; microwaves leased from the commercial telephone companies; special military radio links, some direct, some bounced off the ionosphere, and some channeled through satellites; transmitters with prerecorded messages on board missiles, like ERCS; and even emergency beeping submarine buoys. Each link is vulnerable in its own way, from either sabotage on the ground, jamming by enemy radio, destruction in space through anti-satellite weapons, blackout from electromagentic pulses from nuclear explosions, or even disruptions by natural phenomena, such as storms and sunspot activity. A true picture of the enormity of the commanders' communications problem can only be gained from looking at each of the links in turn, to find out how they can be used and how they are vulnerable.

A normal telephone link converts acoustic signals, such as the human voice, into electrical signals at one end and then turns the electrical signals back into sound at the other. The signals are carried by wires made of a substance such as copper, which can conduct electricity, or of glass fibers through which light can be guided. Such links can carry messages very fast so that there is almost instantaneous reproduction of the message at the other end of the line. These links are admirably suited to communicating with land-based strategic weapons systems. However, such fixed land lines are also extremely vulnerable to attacking missiles, sabotage, or the effects of the electromagnetic pulses created by exploding nuclear weapons. They can really only be counted on in peacetime.

The second broad category of communications is radio. These radio waves are very versatile; they can be received between two stations in several ways. They can be direct, the so-called "line of sight" link, where neither hills nor the curvature of the earth get in the way, or they can be directed skyward and "bounced" off different layers of the atmosphere back to an earth station. In that way the waves can be transmitted over the horizon.

Radio waves range from extremely low frequency to extremely high frequency, known by their acronyms, ELF and EHF, with some of the more familiar wave bands in between such as MF, for medium frequency, and VHF and UHF, for very- and ultra-high frequency. The low-frequency signals are reliable over very long distances, up to several thousands of miles, and are not affected by electromagnetic pulses from nuclear explosions. They can be made resistant to jamming and can penetrate seawater to submarine operating depths. But they have three key disadvantages: They are expensive, they must have huge antennae (several thousand feet, at least), and the messages are transmitted very slowly. If voice messages were transmitted via low frequencies to submarines, for example, they would reach them sounding like a *Star Wars* robot.

The MF band, the normal broadcasting band known in Europe as medium frequency and in America as AM (amplitude modulation), transmits information at higher rates, but the signals do not travel far—up to 100 miles on the ground. The HF, high frequency, or "short wave," radio signals can broadcast voice messages over longer distances by bouncing them off the atmosphere and they are transmitted from smaller antennae requiring much less power to operate. But they are easily "blacked out" for long periods by electro-magnetic pulses (EMP) from nuclear explosions, and the location of the transmitter can be found easily from direction finders. The VHF waves, well known to radio listeners as the ones that produce the best sound, don't travel very far because they are not strongly reflected from the upper atmosphere.

UHF (ultra-high frequency), SHF (super-high frequency), and EHF (extremely high frequency) bands are used in satellite communications, giving excellent reception from very small antennae—SHF and EHF antennae are only about five inches in diameter and can easily be mounted on ground vehicles, aircraft, surface ships, and submarine masts. They too can be "blacked out" by EMP, and the UHF "uplink" to the satellite is fairly easy to jam.

Finally, a third category, lasers, can theoretically produce communications of excellent quality, but the method is far from being fully tested and has its drawbacks. Even in cloudy weather the laser is visible as a pencil-thin ray of light and thus would give away the position of any transmission.

The planners of nuclear war make use of all of these types of communications, setting up systems with names like Giant Talk and Scope Signal, the worldwide HF systems providing the basic means for "positive control" over the nuclear bomber force, or Clarinet Omen, a system for submarine communications. In NATO, the main nuclear command link, an HF radio system, has the ominous title, Cemetery Network. All the systems are part of the Worldwide Military Command and Control System (WWMCCS, or Wimex for short), but those specially designed to survive a nuclear attack are included in a special system called the Minimum Essential Emergency Communications Network (MEECN). Included in MEECN is the network of six very-low frequency navy transmitters, with antenna towers higher than 1,000 feet—taller than the Eiffel Tower—in Washington State, Maine, Maryland, Hawaii, Japan, and Australia. MEECN also includes ERCS, and the airborne command posts, the Cover All and Nightwatch, and the navy's relay plane, TACAMO. The most secret part of MEECN is a special "research" satellite communications link. Two 1,000-pound satellites launched in 1976 operate in near-synchronous orbit following the same track over the surface of the earth while spaced several thousand miles apart. Each can receive communications from a circle on the earth with a diameter of 8,000 miles and they can also communicate with each other. Operating together they can cover more than three-quarters of the earth's surface.

Yet even the highly refined technology used in MEECN does nothing to help solve the main strategic nuclear communications problem: submarines. More than half of the 10,000 strategic warheads in the American stockpile are on submarine-based missiles, and communications between their keepers and the mainland command posts are tenuous. The submarines depend upon a network of VLF stations used to relay messages (submarines on patrol never return calls for fear of exposing their position) and the fleet of specially rigged Hercules C-130 aircraft trailing an antenna six miles long. These TACAMO aircraft remain constantly aloft over the Atlantic and are on alert in the Pacific. To receive messages the submarines tow an antenna about forty feet below the surface, the maximum depth at which the VLF radio waves can be received. The antennae hinder the submarine's movement beneath the surface, limiting its maneuvers and causing a wake in a high-speed run, or a turn, which can be detected by any aircraft using radar or infrared systems that may be on patrol. These deficiencies led the navy to seek another means of communication. It is possible to use laser beams at blue-green wavelengths, either generated aboard satellites or reflected by them from land-based generators, but this method is still at an early stage of development. The system President Reagan favored when outlining his nuclear program in October 1981 is ELF (extremely low frequency) radio waves.

ELF was conceived before the first Polaris missile submarine was put to sea in 1960. The principle is simple: the lower the frequency of the radio wave, the deeper the wave can penetrate into water. Although this principle was known in the 1940s, no one started to look into the possibility of using ELF waves for communications until 1958. In that year a physicist named Nicholas Christofilos, working at the Lawrence Radiation Laboratory at Livermore, California, made some new calculations on what happens to some of the energy released in a nuclear explosion. If a nuclear weapon were fired a few hundred miles above the earth, but within its magnetic field, Christofilos forecasted that high energy particles from the explosion would become trapped in that magnetism and a series of electromagnetic pulses, similar to lightning, would be produced. Three high-altitude nuclear weapons were exploded over the Pacific in 1962 and one of them, over Johnston Island, caused severe electrical malfunctions in Hawaii, 800 miles away. Strings of street lights in Oahu went out and hundreds of burglar alarms in Honolulu were set off when the pulses overloaded their circuits.

These test explosions of nuclear weapons in the atmosphere confirmed the electromagnetic pulse effect. Immediately following a nuclear explosion, air molecules are ionized by gamma rays. The resulting EMPs travel at the speed of light searching out conductors, such as radio aerials or power lines, through which to ground themselves. The high energy from the EMP is received by the antenna in such a short time—less than thousandths of a second—that it can easily damage equipment attached to it. A nuclear explosion of several hundred kilotons (the equivalent of a Minuteman warhead) at 190 miles above the center of the United States would affect communications across the entire American continent including parts of Canada and Mexico.

High-altitude nuclear explosions also change the densities in large regions of the ionosphere, and these changes seriously disrupt all but the longer low frequency radio waves. One of the navy's answers to electromagnetic pulses was ELF. There was a serious problem, however, because the generation of such low frequency waves requires antennae many hundreds of miles long. Christofilo's answer was to use a part of the earth's interior as the antenna.

What was required was a bedrock of granite, a central transmitter, and a few hundred miles of antennae. The current flowing through the granite, a poor conductor, would fan out and act as an excellent wave generator. The Laurentian Highlands (also called the Canadian Shield), a granite mass that spreads south from Canada into northern Michigan and Wisconsin, provided such a site, and in 1968 the navy proposed Project Sanguine, a huge honeycomb of antennae 6,000 miles long buried five feet underground. The snag was that this "antennae farm" would cover 41 percent of the state of Wisconsin.

There was so much public opposition—from concern about soil erosion and wildlife to the fact that Project Sanguine would make Wisconsin an obvious target in any nuclear war—that the navy backed down, making a more modest proposal. The second project, Seafarer, had only 2,400 miles of antennae, this time all aboveground. The navy wooed Michigan politicians to get Seafarer approved. One state legislator was apparently so impressed he was moved to claim that the project would eventually

mean as much to northern Michigan as General Motors
had meant to Detroit. The statement was ludicrous, of
course. Once built, the navy's project would employ a few
hundred workers at most.

Opposition to the project grew and in 1976, while campaigning in Wisconsin, presidential candidate Jimmy
Carter promised that, if elected, Seafarer would never be
built against the wishes of the residents of the state. In
1978, President Carter finally ruled out a full-scale project
of any kind. But, three years later, in October 1981, President Reagan approved a Defense Department recom-
mendation to go ahead with a further reduced project
simply known as ELF. The final site would have 28 miles
of antennae in Wisconsin and 56 miles in Michigan; all of
it would be aboveground. Asked whether this did not
mean the navy was accepting an inferior system because
they couldn't get the one they wanted for environmental
and cost reasons, a navy spokesman replied, "Some system is better than none at all . . . we have gained a capability."

ELF may give the navy a "capability," but it is certainly
not the kind President Reagan's new "war-fighting" orders require. Indeed, the difference between what the
Defense Department has always assumed its C^3I system
had to be able to do and what is now required of it is the
key to understanding the impossible demands of the Reagan nuclear program. In the past, the Defense Department assumed that its C^3I system was set up to give timely
warning of an attack so that the first blow would be survived and a retaliatory strike could be executed. That is

all. The ground command posts have been considered
vulnerable for many years, even those buried deep inside
mountains. Moreover, the C^3I facilities such as the early-
warning radars and the communications have always
been considered targets and unlikely to survive. But the
various Carter presidential directives on nuclear war and
the Reagan administration made some basic changes.

The new C^3I program has its origins in PD-53, covering
national security telecommunications policy; in PD-58,
which lays the ground rules for "continuity" of government after a nuclear war; and PD-59, the order to the
American forces to be able to fight a long nuclear war.
PD-53 and PD-58 are specific orders for improving C^3I.
PD-53 says that it is "essential to the security of the U.S.
to have telecommunications adequate to satisfy the needs
of the nation during and after a national emergency."
This requirement was originally introduced when the National Communications System, the presidential command link, was set up in 1963, but PD-53 also called for
something new: The communications had to be able to
"support flexible execution of retaliatory strikes during
and *after* [emphasis added] an enemy attack." PD-58, like
previous orders for reconvening a national government,
requires the swift evacuation and survival of the Washington leadership, but it also requires this to happen while
successive retaliatory strikes in the SIOP are being implemented and to continue until a successful "termination"
of the war. Admiral James Holloway, chief of naval operations during the Carter administration, summed up the
C^3I challenge thus, "There is nothing more important in
our entire strategic modernization effort . . . than correct-

ing the enduring C^3I problem."

The Reagan administration swiftly endorsed the PDs, the president codifying his own version in National Security Decision Directive Nos. 12 and 13. In closed hearings before the Senate Armed Services Committee in February 1981, a month after Reagan took office, the retiring SAC commander, General Richard Ellis, discussed what specific problems were involved in upgrading the C^3I system. "A major flaw exists," he declared, "in the way our nation manages its massive C^3I network. . . . C^3I is the glue which binds our war fighting capability together," [but it is made up of] essentially soft, fragile peacetime systems."

Here was the real key. The new programs, whatever the Reagan administration would claim, were essentially to prepare the country to *fight* a nuclear war. They fell into three categories: improved early warning, "more survivable command posts," and new communication links. Because C^3I had been neglected for so long, at least some of the new investment was scheduled for purely peacetime, or defensive, programs, including a retaliatory strike, but others were clearly only useful for actually fighting nuclear wars.

In the early-warning category, no one who believes in the retaliatory response of the nuclear deterrent would deny that the systems should be as foolproof as possible. They would not object, for example, to the proposal for six mobile ground terminals to ensure receipt of the signals of an attack from the infrared early-warning satellites that can detect rocket launches. Nor would they object to insuring against deceiving and jamming of those satellites or to the idea that new satellites are worth funding for the late 1980s. But the billions of dollars allocated to building new early-warning stations, upgrading the Dew Line radar sites, and buying twelve new Airborne Warning and Control System (AWACS) flying radar stations will only be adding more vulnerable equipment to a system that already provides excellent warning of an impending attack. Nothing is planned to make this new equipment less vulnerable to attack. The reason given for needing the new ground stations is to improve the "assessment" of the attack—how many missiles there are, where they have come from, and where they are going. Such changes sound innocent enough until the fine print in the Defense Department's justification is studied. These new machines are not needed just for warning; they would also provide precise details of the progress of a nuclear campaign—how many nuclear weapons had exploded and what damage had been done, on both sides. In the words of one air force report the machines would "support the retaliatory process"—however long it lasted.

In the second category, command posts, there are some programs that appear to go against conventional wisdom of what *can* survive, and others that have a certain dreamlike quality to them. One plan, for example, proposes to make certain changes to the airborne command planes (the SAC Cover Alls and the presidential Nightwatch aircraft) so that they can "survive a nuclear attack." Yet congressional documents assert that neither of these planes would "be expected to be available in the aftermath of nuclear exchanges." Defense Secretary Caspar Weinberger has suggested moving the presidential plane farther inland because its present location at Andrews Air

Force Base, just outside Washington, D.C., is too close to the enemy submarine patrol areas. Yet when President Carter tested the system of getting to Andrews in the few minutes available under nuclear attack, he never made it. What would be the use of having a plane even farther away?

In a memorable flight of fancy, still another plan is to provide a secret bunker in a truck for those commanders who survive the destruction of the airborne and ground command posts: The National Command Authority could conduct the leadership of the Western world from an interstate highway!

In the category of new communications, it seems quite logical, in the name of nuclear deterrence, to call for improvements in the communications with submarines, to make sure that the submarine commanders do not launch their missiles by mistake in peacetime and that the West's submarine-based deterrent is credible. But neither the present ELF program nor improvements to the already vulnerable VLF stations will provide that.

A host of "reconstitutable" communications relays, including post-nuclear-war plans to launch new satellites from submarines and even balloons, are clearly a waste of money. The theory is that, after nuclear exchanges in which all communications facilities are destroyed, these so-called "reconstitutable" networks could be swiftly set up. The fact, however, is that there are now enough warheads on both sides to knock out any of these supposed "surviving" assets. Equally unrealistic plans exist for reforming a national government—as if people could survive more easily than underground command posts.

These new proposals are secret; only their code names are known: "Quick Jump," "Greater Slope," "Project Exodus."

Finally, two satellite projects have especially sinister overtones. One is MILSTAR, a new interservice satellite system providing two-way, jam-resistant communications operating at extremely high frequencies (EHF). It is supposed to add to, and eventually replace, a perfectly good air force satellite communications system, known as AFSATCOM, which has only been operating since 1974. AFSATCOM has receivers aboard bombers, reconnaissance aircraft, and submarines and in command posts and missile launch control centers. In 1983 the system will be fully operational with some 900 terminals. MILSTAR will, in theory, use new, small EHF terminals and antennae and will allow communications between all armed services using both strategic and tactical nuclear weapons. According to the Defense Department it is also designed "to provide survivable and enduring command and control . . . through all levels of conflict, including general nuclear war." But even the defense intellectuals have their doubts. The Mitre Corporation's Charles Zraket says, "It would have been nice since military satellites are very important for all functions of C^3I, if a few hundred million dollars more were available to upgrade what we already have. The problem with EHF is that we are not going to get a fully deployed system with a full suite of 3,000 terminals for 10 to 15 years."

The second satellite system, code named Forest Green and known as the Integrated Operational Nuclear Detection System (IONDS), is a set of eighteen nuclear explosion detectors riding piggyback on navigational satellites. Their sole job is to locate and report nuclear detonations around the world during a nuclear war. They are a more sophisticated version of the two Vela satellites already in operation searching for so-called peaceful, or experimental, nuclear explosions such as the test conducted by India in 1974. The Forest Green satellites are not intended for peacetime application; they will be used only during an extended nuclear war to help the generals redirect their missiles if the targets they are already aimed at have been blown up.

So, will the new gadgets work? Even if they do "work," they will not improve protection against a nuclear war. A 1982 study on C^3I "endurance" by the Carnegie Endowment for International Peace observed that the new C^3I programs "certainly [do] not mean that the United States should have complete confidence that the C^3I system could perform all its functions without impairment after attack. The power of nuclear weapons and the uncertainty of effects, both physical and psychological, of a nuclear exchange make that an unattainable goal." And a 1981 Congressional Budget Office report concluded, "Technologically sophisticated systems designed to enhance responsiveness are unlikely to survive to function for long periods after a nuclear attack." The CBO, the congressional adviser on budget alternatives, invited the politicians to choose between "C^3I modernization on responsiveness or on endurance, or whether to stress both objectives by pursuing both courses simultaneously."

If what the experts say is true—that the technology cannot make the systems more survivable—and yet "warfighting" machines such as IONDS are built, the net effect could ultimately be to increase the influence of the military in any decision to use nuclear weapons. It would work like this. The military, with their highly sophisticated sensors and computers giving them immediate information of events as they happen, would be able to present persuasive arguments to the president about what he should do next by asserting that their information has more relevance than any political considerations.

To understand presidential control, a distinction must be made between what the military can do and what the rules say they should do. Today, it is physically possible for high-level military officers to circumvent the system and launch nuclear weapons without a presidential order. Submarine commanders can launch their missiles should they lose contact with national command authorities following a nuclear attack. Procedures have also been established permitting officers at airborne command posts—the flying bunkers—to authorize the launching of missiles and bombers should they be the highest level of command surviving a nuclear attack.

Officially, the military will never be given more autonomy in decisions on the use of nuclear weapons, but whether they are or not will matter less and less. The new C^3I system, with its emphasis on vulnerability of the command and control mechanisms, will serve to narrow the options of whoever is in charge, whoever has survived. A single response will be built into the structure of the system: to shoot. Today's nuclear battlefield no longer allows the luxury of presidential control; there will be no breathing spaces during which a responsible decision could be made. If it is true, as the generals say, that the technology of nuclear weapons has now evolved to the point where the greatest danger is that the leadership itself will be destroyed, then, in planning our response to a Soviet nuclear attack, we have come full circle to automatic massive retaliation or nothing. There is no flexibility in the system anymore.

EPILOGUE

Degrading Gracefully

"The victor [in a nuclear war] may well be the man who blinds his enemy and destroys his command and control facilities faster than his own are degraded . . . the challenge [is] devising systems which will be resistant to enemy attack and which will degrade gracefully . . . after the initial clash."—James Wade, Principal Under Secretary of Defense for Research and Engineering, April 1982

THE lexicon of nuclear deterrence has become steadily more bewildering as each American administration has tried to give a more acceptable cast to nuclear war. In the 1950s it was simple and straightforward. The massive retaliation doctrine of the Eisenhower years could not have been clearer: Any attack would receive a single devastating response. In the 1960s MacNamara's doctrine of mutual assured destruction, with its unintentional acronym MAD left no doubts that both sides could obliterate each other. But MAD added to a stream of terms befuddling even to those familiar with military jargon—

terms such as counterforce, countervalue, and damage limitation. Like much of the military's language, these were catchwords for whole concepts of how to do battle, and they always required further explanation and interpretation.

Through the 1970s the declared policy of deterrence again went through major changes, adding still more catchwords. There was Nixon's doctrine of sufficiency and controlled response, and Jimmy Carter's countervailing strategy, all seeking to tailor deterrence doctrine so that everyone—the politicians, the military establishment, and the citizenry—could be comfortable with it. By 1981, the old concept of mutual destruction had been called so many new things that it was no longer clear whether deterrence assumed the worst: Nuclear weapons had become so "refined" that they could now be used in small, "limited" wars that did not threaten massive destruction.

The Reagan White House opened with a new national security team vowing to put its own stamp on America's defense policies, but there was no need for yet another perplexing buzzword. Jimmy Carter had left a "deterrence" strategy in place so close to war fighting that it suited the Republican promise of "nuclear superiority." Carter may have spoken softly about peace and warned during the 1980 presidential campaign against choosing a belligerent alternative in Ronald Reagan, but his "countervailing strategy" had made the final break with deterrence through assured destruction by actually calling on the American forces to be able to fight a prolonged nuclear war, one that could last for months, instead of the few hours or days everyone had always expected. The Carter doctrine, embodied in the executive order PD-59, was swiftly embraced by the new Reagan team, with one important addition. Reagan said that American nuclear forces had to be able not only to fight a prolonged nuclear war, but also to *prevail.*

The single word "prevail" was to cause quite a stir— fueling the fears of many that Ronald Reagan, the ex-Hollywood cowboy, suffered from an itchy trigger finger. To prevail in a nuclear war meant to win. Even though the military's top generals accepted that there could be no "winners" in a nuclear war, the loose-lipped Reagan defense team sounded disturbingly confident about the concept of nuclear victory.

Defense Secretary Caspar Weinberger declared, "If a war is not serious enough for us to want to win, it is not serious enough for us to enter . . . I hope we will never again become involved in another war unless we mean to win it." His deputy, Frank Carlucci, observed, "I think we need to have a counterforce capability. Over and above that, I think that we need to have a war-fighting capability." Navy secretary John Lehman was unequivocal, "You have to have a war-winning capability if you are to succeed." The SAC commander, General Bennie Davis, told Congress in 1982 that the United States had dropped the policy of mutual assured destruction "at least two years ago" and that the policy was "counterforce" or "war fighting"—"the two are synonymous."

And so it went on down the line of Reagan officials. James Wade, principal under secretary of defense, a former member of the Carter team, and a man with an unnerving proclivity for chilling comments, laid it out as clearly as any military official when he said, "We don't want to fight a nuclear war, or a conventional one either, but we must be prepared to do so if such a battle is to be deterred, as we must also be prepared to carry the battle to our adversary's homeland. We must not fear war."

Not even nuclear war, apparently. Here, finally, was a team not afraid to tell the world the cold, hard facts of nuclear war policy. They were saying what no one else had dared to mention for more than two decades, that no nation has contingency plans to lose wars, even nuclear ones. Under Reagan there was to be no more pussyfooting around pretending that the United States did not have a plan to blow the Soviet Union off the edge of the earth; no more of the elegant, liberal, intellectual analyses of deterrence by "decent" and "sensible" men trying to craft the concept of nuclear deterrence into something universally acceptable, even "humane"; no more talk of sparing cities and only targeting the enemy's "war making facilities," their missiles, their military forces, and their factories. The Reagan administration invoked no such nuclear niceties; they had come to the point where destruction of everything that had been targeted before —and more—was necessary to deter the Russians. The Soviet leadership in their secret bunkers would be on the target list; "prevailing" in a nuclear war would require the very roots of the communist state to be destroyed. That was what today's nuclear deterrence was about. The 1980s would be the decade of straight talk about nuclear weapons and especially about nuclear wars. "I'm frankly uncertain on just what [our critics] think our defense planning should have been based," said navy secretary, John Lehman; "the only alternatives that come readily to mind are planning to fight but not to prevail or not preparing to fight at all, which is precisely what we have been doing with the defense cutting in recent years."

The great irony of President Reagan's saber-rattling is that when he tried to frighten the Soviets about U.S. military belligerence, he also scared the wits out of the American and European people. When the public outcry came, the president and his team complained that they had been misunderstood: They had only told the truth about the things previous administrations had kept intentionally confusing and fuzzy. Certainly, they were only doing what all other administrations had done—"improving" the war plan in the name of "improving" deterrence. Defense Secretary Weinberger claimed to be miffed by all the newspaper accounts portraying the administration as nuclear "war fighters" and, in August 1982, he took the unusual step of writing a letter of explanation to some forty editors of major newspapers in America and in Europe.

The newspapers were wrong, said Weinberger. The administration did not believe there could be any "winners" in a nuclear war. The earlier thoughts and pronouncements of the Reagan team were conveniently forgotten. Weinberger proclaimed that the administration's strategy was the same as it had been for all previous administrations, namely, to deter war of all kinds, but most particularly to deter nuclear war. "Since the awful age of nuclear weapons began," he wrote, "the United States has sought to prevent war through a policy of deterrence. This policy has been approved, through the political processes of the democratic nations it protects, since at least 1950."

Yet one of the first lessons in our examination of the SIOP is that United States strategic nuclear policy was never "approved" by any part of the democratic process;

indeed, all nuclear weapons programs in the three Western nuclear-armed countries—the United States, Britain, and France—were conceived and nurtured in the greatest secrecy. In America, there is even a document to prove it, National Security Council Document No. 30 of September 1948. This document, which we discuss in Chapter 2, decreed that the United States would maintain peace and security, using atomic weapons if necessary, and that the ultimate decision to fire them would be the president's. On no account was this basic policy decision to be discussed in public, and at no time since have the normal checks and balances of the democratic process been involved in any refinements of the deterrence concept. In short, politicians, generals, and defense intellectuals have proclaimed that new weapons, or new doctrines, are needed to "ensure" deterrence, and the public has acquiesced in their masquerade.

Second, Weinberger proclaimed something that was all too familiar: The United States had to have a "warfighting" nuclear force because that's what the Russians are doing. The Russians, said Weinberger, are building forces for a "protracted" conflict; to have a "credible" deterrence the United States has to do the same. No one denies the formidable nature of the Soviet nuclear forces; yet, after the "bomber gap" and the "missile gap" we have learned to be suspicious of new military programs based on estimates of the threat.

Weinberger's use of the threat was no election ploy, however. How to keep America safe from the "advancing communist hordes" was a genuine preoccupation of the new administration. There was Richard Pipes, the Har-

vard professor of Russian history, who became Reagan's
senior adviser on Soviet and Eastern European affairs, a
critical national security post. Pipes selected passages
from Soviet nuclear strategies of nuclear war fighting,
reinforcing the president's notion that it was necessary for
America to prepare likewise. The sages, like Pipes, conveniently left out things the president might not want to
hear, such as that the Soviet strategists also talk of the
"unacceptability" of a world nuclear war and of "the ne-
cessity for its prevention."

Such omissions are enough to make us all feel uneasy
about the "rationale" that drives the current version of
deterrence, but there is more. The new deterrence envi-
sions limited wars, something that veteran nuclear strategists had dismissed as impossible years before. However,
President Reagan, in his own fumbling fashion, told a
stunned world that he thought such wars were possible.
"Do you believe," Reagan was asked by a journalist in
October 1981, "that there could be a limited exchange of
nuclear weapons between us and the Soviet Union or that
it would simply escalate inevitably?" President Reagan
replied, "I don't honestly know. I think . . . [that] all over
the world there is . . . research going on to try to find the
defensive weapons. There never has been a weapon
. . . [for which] someone hasn't come up with a defense.
But it could . . . [happen] and the only defense is, you shoot
yours and we'll shoot ours. And if you . . . still have that
kind of [nuclear] stalemate, I could see where you could
have the exchange of tactical weapons in the field without
it bringing either one of the major powers to pushing the
button."

After the homilies of the Carter years such nuclear
bombast was so startling it appeared that the Reagan administration had thought of something totally new. In
fact, the United States had come full circle. In the 1950s
when the war plan was in the hands of generals like
LeMay, there was never any question of fighting without
winning. It was declared national policy to win. No one,
not even the politicians, tried to maintain otherwise. In a
1956 article in *Foreign Affairs,* Paul Nitze, a leading expo-
nent of Cold War politics and at present a Reagan arms
negotiator, had argued that, despite the eventual equality
between East and West in nuclear armaments, it would
still be possible for there to be a "decisive" winner when
the word "win" is "used to suggest a comparison of the
postwar position of one of the adversaries with the postwar position of the other adversary . . . [because] the
victor will be in a position to issue orders to the loser and
the loser will have to obey them or face complete chaos
or extinction."

At the time that it was made, this statement was one of
the more cold-blooded assessments about nuclear war,
and when the officials of the Reagan administration re-
peat it today, it is no less chilling. It is also misguided and
dangerous. In 1956 it was certainly possible to imagine, as
Nitze did, that the superior forces of the United States
could have turned the Soviet Union into a vast dust bowl
while escaping a similar fate, but as the Soviet nuclear
forces grew this vision became less of a reality. With
today's weapons systems it is hard to imagine how anyone
could base nuclear policy on the possibility of surviving a
nuclear war. Over the years, "rational" politicians have

asked for "options" in the war plans in an illusory effort to "prevent" full-scale wars and to make the U.S. deterrent more credible by showing a willingness to use nuclear weapons. The options grew with the increasing numbers of nuclear weapons available to the war planners. Today, the SIOP has reached the point where it contains so many options to bolster "deterrence" that it is no different from any conventional contingency war plans. The current war-fighting strategy begs the question: How will a limited nuclear war be terminated before large-scale destruction has occurred? Yet the technical and political difficulties of "escalation control" and "war termination," as the jargon goes, have never been properly addressed. The "hot-line" telex machine, for example, sits in the Pentagon in a "soft" command post where the planners assume it will be destroyed. The problems of getting the political leadership, on either side, into command bunkers that will survive the first round of a nuclear exchange and enable those leaders to communicate with each other are unsolvable. The only way to overcome the problems, as the Pentagon's James Wade makes clear, is to have a system that "degrades gracefully."

"Graceful degradation" would occur on two fronts: with the weapons and with communications systems. Following Carter's lead in PD-59, the Reagan planners are developing what the strategists call a "second-strike counterforce capability." This means having missiles, such as the larger MX and the more accurate Trident II, that can survive a total attack from the Soviet Union. Such survivable missiles will be launched during the "trans-attack" and "post-attack" periods, which range from a few days to a few months. As the rest of the nuclear force and the nation disintegrates, this "secure reserve force" is due to ensure victory.

To make these weapons more credible, the Reagan administration launched the largest-ever C^3I program—but, as we have shown in Chapter 10, there is considerable scepticism among the experts as to whether any amount of investment would produce a communications system able to endure a nuclear attack. Already the amount of money being spent to execute the options means that C^3I has become a separate and limitless part of the arms race. There may be no way of perfecting communications, but as long as the war-fighting policy requirement exists there is no limit to the number of new options that will be created in trying to reach such perfection.

In the process, the planners will be searching for a technology that gives them more time to make their response to a Soviet missile attack. What will happen? The planners will continue to give the impression that C^3I can somehow ensure the continuity of civilian control over nuclear weapons from peacetime to wartime. In peacetime, as we have said, it is hard to argue against further "upgrades" in control, such as keeping pace with weapons safety or computer technology. The politicians and the military can "prove" that, in peacetime, the C^3I system works, as they did during the false alerts at SAC headquarters and NORAD in June 1980. However, to comply with "the letter as well as the spirit" of PD-59, as ex-commander of SAC General Richard Ellis observed, they have to try to create a communications and command system that will control the course of a nuclear war, and time is their most persistent problem. No matter what the war planners do, the presidential decision time after a surprise attack on Washington, D.C., from a Soviet missile submarine in the Atlantic is fixed at less than ten minutes. For an intercontinental missile, it will always be about thirty minutes. Presidential decision time will remain the same, as will the president's ability to survive the attack, even as the number of response options increases.

In a nuclear exchange the new early-warning satellites and communications stations being built specifically for war fighting would give the generals sitting in the command bunkers an extraordinary amount of instant information about the battle being fought many thousands of miles away. New methods of retargeting missiles and bombers permit almost endless varieties of responses to nuclear attack. The generals would have a great advantage over their commander in chief, the president, in being able to draw up "options" that the politicians might never have foreseen. After all, the options set forth in the president's black SIOP books rely on theoretical attack patterns and theoretical responses, and one of the things we can be sure about a nuclear war is that it would not go according to plan.

In the present SIOP, only one choice before the president is still convincing. That choice is the Major Attack Option, releasing more than a thousand warheads in a single strike against Soviet forces. It is the same option that was open to the president in the 1950s. All the limited options, which are subject to the generals' instant interpretations, have as their purpose fighting and winning.

Today's Single Integrated Operational Plan is no longer a *single* plan for ensuring deterrence; it is a mere symbol of a bygone age when being able to coordinate the threat of a massive nuclear response was thought to be good enough to deter the Soviet Union.

Glossary

Airborne command posts: a flying command post, converted from commercial aircraft with special communications and used as flying bunkers; includes the National Emergency Airborne Command Post (NEACP), code named "Nightwatch," for the President, Joint Chiefs of Staff, and Commander of the Strategic Air Command; the Post Attack Command and Control System (PACCS), code named "Cover All" or "Looking Glass," for Strategic Air Command; and regional command posts—"Silk Purse" for European Command, "Blue Eagle" for Pacific Command, and "Scope Light" for Atlantic Command.

Bombers: long-range or heavy bombers are those capable of traveling 6,000 or more miles on one load of fuel; medium-range or medium bombers can travel between 3,500 and 6,000 miles without refueling.

Command centers: the nerve center of military operations. Information from early-warning sensors, intelligence collection, and military and political sources is assessed, and responses are formulated and transmitted. U.S. national level command centers include the National Military Command Center in the Pentagon, the Alternate National Military Command Center in Raven Rock in southern Pennsylvania, the SAC underground command post at Offutt Air Force base in Nebraska, and the

NORAD underground command post inside Cheyenne Mountain in Colorado.

Communications intelligence (COMINT): intelligence collected from intercepting voice communications, over radios, satellites, and so forth.

Counterforce: the use of nuclear weapons (used to describe strategies, attacks, weapons, and so forth) against an opponent's military forces and industry.

Countervalue: the use of nuclear weapons (used to describe strategies, attacks, weapons, and so forth) against an opponent's civilian and economic centers.

Defense Readiness Conditions (DEFCONs): the state of alert of U.S. military forces, ranging from Defense Condition 5, the lowest, to Defense Condition 1:

DEFCON 5: normal readiness

DEFCON 4: increased intelligence watch and strengthened security measures

DEFCON 3: an increase in force readiness above that required for normal readiness

DEFCON 2: a further increase in readiness but less than maximum readiness

DEFCON 1: maximum force readiness

Deterrence: the dissuasion of a potential adversary from initiating an attack or conflict, mostly by the threat of unacceptable retaliatory damage.

Early warning: in the strategic sense it is the interception, via radar or infrared means, of the launch of aircraft or missiles.

Electronics intelligence (ELINT): intelligence collected from intercepting radar signals and other nonvoice communications.

Emergency Action Message (EAM): the means by which an order to use nuclear weapons is passed from the National Command Authorities to the forces.

Federal Emergency Management Agency (FEMA): the agency of the government responsible for civil defense and the continuity of government.

First strike: the initial attack with nuclear weapons in which the attacker attempts to destroy all or a large portion of its adversary's strategic nuclear forces before they can be launched.

FLASH: the highest precedence for expediting communications from the field to the national command authorities and vice versa.

Football: the black briefcase containing the nuclear weapons release codes and attack options carried by a military aide to the president.

Hot line: the permanent, open telex link between Washington and Moscow.

Joint Emergency Evacuation Plan (JEEP): the plan for evacuating a select number (about 250) military and civilian government employees in time of nuclear war.

Joint Strategic Target Planning Staff (JSTPS): the joint staff of the air force, navy, army, marine corps, and representatives of NATO allies that plans strategic nuclear force allocations to enemy targets listed in the SIOP.

Launch control center (LCC): the underground command posts used to launch land-based missiles.

Launch on Warning (LOW): a condition under which bombers and missiles would be launched on receipt of early warning that an opponent has launched his missiles.

Launch under Attack (LUA): a condition where the early-warning information received on the launch of an opponent's missiles is confirmed and bombers and missiles are launched to survive an attack.

Minimum Essential Emergency Communications Network (MEECN): the network of low-frequency, satellite, and airborne communications systems expected to survive an attack and remain to pass on retaliatory commands to strategic forces.

Missiles: those with a range of 4,000 or more miles are called intercontinental ballistic missiles; those with a range of between 1,500 and 4,000 nautical miles are called intermediate-range ballistic missiles.

Mutual assured destruction (MAD): a doctrine of reciprocal deterrence that rests on the ability of two opponents to inflict unacceptable damage on one another after surviving a nuclear first strike.

National Command Authority (NCA): the president and the secretary of defense or their duly deputized stand-ins or successors. The chain of command runs from the president to the secretary of defense and through the Joint Chiefs of Staff to the commanders of the regional and specified commands.

NUCFLASH: a report used to provide the National Command authorities with immediate notification of accidental or unauthorized launchings of a nuclear weapon that could create risk of outbreak of war with the Soviet Union.

Nuclear weapon: a general name given to any weapon in which the explosion results from the energy released by reactions involving atomic nuclei. There are 26,000 nuclear weapons in the U.S. arsenal, and approximately 18,000 in the Soviet arsenal.

PD-59: President Carter's three-page guidance to the military for nuclear war preparedness.

Real time: information received in "real time" means the instant an event occurs it is recorded by intelligence sensors and transmitted to operational units.

Reconnaissance aircraft: any aircraft equipped with intelligence collecting apparatus, such as special cameras, radar, or listening devices.

Satellites: military satellites are used to detect missile launches, collect intelligence information, and communicate with forces around the world. The first ones were launched in the late 1950s.

Security classification: the method of restricting national security data ranging from confidential to secret and top secret. At the top of the scale there are some special compartmentalized access clearances, such as extremely sensitive information (ESI) for the SIOP.

Semiautomated Ground Environment (SAGE): a network of air defense command centers that were built in the late 1950s to correlate information from radars on enemy aircraft and to direct interceptor aircraft against them.

Signals intelligence (SIGINT): intelligence collected from intercepting electronic signals, whether communications (COMINT), telemetry (TELINT), or noncommunications electronic (ELINT).

Single Integrated Operational Plan (SIOP): the central nuclear war plan of the United States.

Strategic: a nation's offensive and defensive military potential, including its geographic location and its economic, political, and military strength. Strategic weapons and forces are those capable of directly affecting another nation's strategic position and war-fighting capacity.

Strategic Air Command (SAC): the specified command of the Joint Chiefs of Staff having control over land-based missiles and long-range bombers.

Submarines: There are three generations of strategic submarines with ballistic missiles: Polaris, Poseidon, and Trident.

TACAMO: the radio relay airplane of the navy that is the primary means of communicating with submarines.

Telemetry intelligence (TELINT): intelligence collected from intercepting the electronic signals transmitted by missiles and satellites to earth.

Theater: a geographical area designated for administrative, logistical, and command convenience in which a war would be fought under a single command.

Two-man rule: a procedure designed to prohibit access by one individual to nuclear weapons and release codes by requiring the presence at all times of at least two authorized persons.

Weapons System Evaluation Group (WSEG): an organization in the department of defense set up in the early 1960s to evaluate weapons programs and military alternatives.

Worldwide Military Command and Control System (WWMCCS): the system that provides the means for operational direction and technical administrative support involved in the function of command and control of U.S. military forces.

Acronyms

ABCA	America, Britain, Canada, Australia
ADP	automatic data processing
AEC	Atomic Energy Commission
AFSATCOM	Air Force Satellite Communications System
AWACS	Airborne Warning and Control System
BMEWS	Ballistic Missile Early Warning System
CBO	Congressional Budget Office
C^3I	C-cubed-I
CIA	Central Intelligence Agency
CINCEUR	commander in chief, Europe
CINCLANT	commander in chief, the Atlantic region
COMINT	communications intelligence
CONUS	continental United States
DCA	Defense Communications Agency
DEFCON	Defense Condition
DMZ	demilitarized zone
DSP	Defense Support Program
EAM	emergency action message
EHF	extremely high frequency
ELF	extremely low frequency
ELINT	electronics intelligence
EMP	electro-magnetic pulses

259

EOB	electronic order of battle
ERCS	Emergency Rocket Communications System
ESC	Electronics Security Command (air force)
ESI	extremely sensitive information
EUCOM	European Command
FBM	Fleet Ballistic Missile submarine
FEMA	Federal Emergency Management Agency
GAO	General Accounting Office
ICBM	intercontinental ballistic missile
INSCOM	Intelligence and Security Command (army)
IONDS	Integrated Operational Nuclear Detection System
IRBM	intermediate-range ballistic missile
JCS	Joint Chiefs of Staff
JEEP	Joint Emergency Evacuation Program
JSTPS	Joint Strategic Target Planning Staff
KT	kiloton
LCC	launch control center
LF	low frequency
LAO	limited attack options
LOW	Launch on Warning
LUA	Launch under Attack
MAD	mutual assured destruction
MAO	major attack options
MEECN	Minimal Essential Emergency Communications Network
MF	medium frequency
MIDAS	Missile Detection and Alarm System
MILSTAR	Military Strategic and Tactical Relay System
MIT	Massachusetts Institute of Technology
MT	megaton
MX	missile experimental
NATO	North Atlantic Treaty Organization
NCA	National Command Authority
NEACP	National Emergency Airborne Command Post
NIE	National Intelligence Estimate
NMCC	National Military Command Center

NORAD	North American Aerospace Defense Command
NSA	National Security Agency
NSC	National Security Council
NSDM	National Security Decision Memorandum
NSG	Naval Security Group
NSTL	National Strategic Target List
NUDET	nuclear detonation report
NUDETS	nuclear detection system
NUWEP	Nuclear Weapons Employment Policy
OPLAN	operations plan
OPREP	operational report
PACOM	Pacific Command
PD	presidential directive
PFIAB	President's Foreign Intelligence Advisory Board
PRF	pulse repitition frequency
RAF	Royal Air Force
REDCOM	Readiness Command
RF	radio frequency
RNO	regional nuclear options
SAC	Strategic Air Command
SAGE	Semiautomatic Ground Environment
SALT	Strategic Arms Limitation Talks
SAMOS	Satellite and Missile Observation System
SAO	selected attack options
SHF	super-high frequency
SI	special intelligence
SIGINT	signals intelligence
SIOP	Single Integrated Operational Plan
SRAM	short-range attack missile
SSBN	strategic submarine ballistic nuclear
TACAMO	"Take charge and move out"
TELINT	telemetry intelligence
TNT	trinitrotoluene
TS	top secret
UHF	ultra-high frequency
VHF	very-high frequency

VLF	very-low frequency
WISC	warning systems controller
WSEG	Weapon Systems Evaluation Group
WWMCCS	World Wide Military Command and Control System

Notes and Bibliography

THE literature on the SIOP is sparse. There is considerable detail on the early war plans, particularly before 1953 because that material has largely been declassified in America under the mandatory thirty-year rule. However, much of what we have put together for the subsequent SIOP years has come from interviews with armed forces personnel, either active or retired; use of obscure and recondite military reports, regulations, and manuals; and visits, official briefings, and conversations with military and political experts. The best way of presenting the small amount of important published material is in the form of an essay for each chapter, including the most recently published works relating directly to the government's war plan and its supporting cast of command centers, communications links, and early-warning radar sites. We have not attempted to give more than a brief list of the mass of books and articles on nuclear strategy that have appeared during the last five years.

There are a number of general sources that are useful for understanding the machinery of nuclear weapons command and control. The many military trade magazines of the electronics industry—*Defense Electronics, Military Electronics/Countermeasures, Journal of Electronic Defense, Signal,* and

IEEE Spectrum—and the annual July issue of *Air Force Magazine* on "The Electronic Air Force," all contain intimate details about communications and electronics developments. The best single magazine, and most well known, *Aviation Week & Space Technology,* was the source of much information. In addition, we cannot stress enough the importance of congressional hearings on the Defense Department budget, which have provided a continuing and in-depth examination of military strategy and command, control, and communications programs. Finally, the annual reports of the Department of Defense to Congress, and the research and development reports of the Department, have been reviewed from 1947 to the present. They chronicle the evolution of all aspects of the military since the end of the Second World War.

1: Cocked Pistol

The exercise Ivy League was described in a single major news article, Fialka, John J., "Nuclear Reaction: U.S. Tests Response to an Atomic Attack," *Wall Street Journal,* 26 March 1982. The OPREP system of military reporting that was used in the exercise is described in detail in Joint Chiefs of Staff publications: *Joint Reporting Structure,* JCS Publication 6; *General Instructions,* Vol. I, June 1977; and *Joint Reports,* Vol. II, Pt. 3, "Event/Incident Reports," November 1980. The emergency evacuation system of the government is described in U.S. Department of Defense, *Continuity of Operations Policies and Planning,* Directive No. 3020.26, 22 January 1982. The nuclear detonations reporting system is discussed in *Pacific Command Nuclear Biological Chemical Warning and Reporting System,* Pacific Commander-in-Chief Instruction 3401.3J, 6 February 1981.

2: Incipient Power

The basic sources were two papers written by the American historian David Rosenberg, who has done by far the most comprehensive work on the early nuclear war plans. They are:

David Alan Rosenberg, "A Smoking Radiating Ruin at the End of Two Hours: Documents on American War Plans for Nuclear War with the Soviet Union 1954–55," *International Security*, Vol. 6, No. 3, Winter 1981/82; David Alan Rosenberg, "The Origins of Overkill: Nuclear Weapons and American Strategy 1945–1960," *International Security*, Vol. 7, No. 4, Spring 1983. Other material of Rosenberg's was also useful: the chapter "American Postwar Air Doctrine and Organization: The Navy Experience," in *Air Power and Warfare, Proceedings of the 8th Military History Symposium, United States Air Force Academy 18–20 October 1978*, edited by Alfred Hurley and Robert Ehrhart, Washington, D.C., Office of Air Force History, Headquarters USAF and United States Air Force Academy, 1979; the chapter "Arleigh Burke: The Chief of Naval Operations" edited by Robert William Love, Annapolis, Md., Naval Institute Press, 1980.

On Strategic Air Command and Offutt Air Force Base: There are some very helpful fact sheets published by SAC that give basic information and they are available from the Public Affairs Office on the base. The public is also admitted to limited tours of the command post.

On General LeMay: His biography is, Curtis LeMay, with MacKinley Kantor, *Mission with LeMay; My Story*, Garden City, N.Y., Doubleday, 1965; also, open hearings before U.S. Congress, Senate Committee on Armed Services, Nomination of General Curtis E. LeMay: *87th Congress, 1st Session, On Nomination of LeMay for Appointment as Chief of Staff, Air Force, 8 June 1961*, Washington, D.C., U.S. GPO, 1961. Articles and interviews: "Curtis LeMay," *This Week Magazine*, N.Y., 1962; "Curtis LeMay," *National Observer*, 23 December 1972; interview in *Washington Post*, 31 January 1965; interview with John Bohn, SAC historian, 9 March 1971. The Bohn interview, available from SAC HQ, was especially interesting.

For the early development of the atomic bomb under Truman and his relationship with Congress and the military, see Peter Pringle and James Spigelman, *The Nuclear Barons*, London, Michael Joseph, 1981; Richard Hewlett and Francis

Duncan, *Atomic Shield, A History of the United States Atomic Energy Commission,* Vol 2, U.S. Atomic Energy Commission, Washington, D.C., 1972.

3: The Vacuum Cleaner

Much of the secrecy surrounding the strategic importance of intelligence collection is being broken down due to some excellent investigative and academic studies. The three most significant and useful recent works are: James Bamford, *The Puzzle Palace: A Report on NSA, America's Most Secret Agency,* Boston, Houghton Mifflin, 1982; John Prados, *The Soviet Estimate: U.S. Intelligence Analysis and Russian Military Strength,* New York, Dial Press, 1982; Lawrence Freedman, *U.S. Intelligence and the Soviet Strategic Thought,* London, Macmillan, 1977.

On the U-2 program, see: David Wise and Thomas B. Ross, *The U-2 Affair,* New York, Random House, 1962; Francis Gary Powers, *Operation Overflight,* New York, Holt, Rinehart and Winston, 1970; SSgt. Craig Pugh, "Surviving in High Places," *Airman,* September 1982; Donald E. Fink, "Role of U-2 High-Altitude Surveillance Aircraft to Be Expanded," *Aviation Week & Space Technology,* 16 June 1980. On the SR-71, see: Robert R. Ropelewski, "SR-71 Impressive in High-Speed Regime," *Aviation Week & Space Technology,* 18 May 1981; and "Lockheed's Lone Ranger: Reconnoitering at Mach 3," *Air International,* October 1974. On the RC-135 and other aerial reconnaissance operations, see also: Howard Silbur, "SAC Spy Plane Escaped 'Kidnap,' " *Omaha World-Herald,* 1 October 1980; Jay Miller, "Surveillance Boosted for Iran-Iraq War," *Air Force Times,* 27 October 1980; Alexander Scott (pseudonym), "Crossroads for Strategic Reconnaissance," *Armed Forces Journal International,* May 1979; Howard Silbur, "Task for SAC under SALT Grows with Monitor Losses," *Omaha World-Herald,* 6 May 1979.

The debate on the adequacy of intelligence capabilities for arms control treaty verification has also revealed information about the collection of information on the Soviet Union. The most important sources are: Mark Lowenthal, SALT *Verification*, Congressional Research Service, Library of Congress, 10 July 1978; Robert Kaiser, "Verification of SALT II: Art and Science" (three-part series), *Washington Post*, 15–17 June 1979; Amron Katz, *Verification and SALT: The State of the Art and the Art of the State*, The Heritage Foundation, Washington, D.C., 1979; Rep. Les Aspin, "The Verification of the SALT II Agreement," *Scientific American*, February 1979; "SALT II: Verification," *Mershon Center Quarterly Report*, Summer 1979; Jan M. Lodal, "Verifying SALT," *Foreign Policy*, Fall 1978; Strobe Talbott, "Scrambling and Spying in SALT II," *International Security*, Fall 1979; Ted Greenwood, "Reconnaissance and Arms Control," *Scientific American*, February 1973.

4: The Defenders

Most of the information on early-warning programs comes from North American Aerospace Defense Command (NORAD) and Strategic Air Command (SAC), and from U.S. Department of Defense annual reports. An excellent review of the history of air defense and the evolution of electronics in defense by the Mitre Corporation (*Mitre: The First Twenty Years*, Bedford, Mass., 1979) provides a good overview.

A number of detailed historical reports provide excellent background information: Space Division, History Office, *Space and Missile System Organization: A Chronology, 1954–1979;* Historical Division, U.S. Air Force Electronics Systems Division, *History of the Electronics Systems Division*, Vols. I and II, SAGE: *Background and Origins*, December 1964, both declassified. These reports provide an enormous amount of background material on the evolution of electronics and command and control programs.

On early-warning satellites and space, see: U.S. Arms Control and Disarmament Agency, "Strategic Warning and Attack Assessment," in U.S. Congress, *Arms Control Impact Statements;* "Military Use of Space," in the *Stockholm International Peace Research Institute (SIPRI) Yearbook 1982*, and see previous annual issues; David Baker, *The Shape of Wars to Come,* London, Hamlyn Paperbacks, 1981; John W.R. Taylor and David Mondey, *Spies in the Sky,* London, Ian Allen, 1972; Philip J. Klass, *Secret Sentries in Space,* New York, Random House, 1971.

On air defense and early-warning systems: *Mitre: The First Twenty Years,* Bedford, Mass., Mitre Corp., 1979; 96th U.S. Congress, 1st session, Committee on Armed Services, House of Representitives, *Full Committee Hearing on Continental Air Defense,* 22 July 1981; Clarence A. Robinson, "Strategic Defense Draws Strong Focus," *Aviation Week & Space Technology,* 13 April 1981; Clarence A. Robinson, "Improved U.S. Warning Net Spurred," *Aviation Week & Space Technology,* 23 June 1980; Clarence A. Robinson, "Space Surveillance Deemed Inadequate," *Aviation Week & Space Technology,* 16 June 1980.

5: SIOP-62

As in Chapter 2, by far the best historical paper detailing the events leading up to the first SIOP is David A. Rosenberg's: "The Origins of Overkill: Nuclear Weapons and American Strategy 1945–1960," *International Security,* Vol. 7, No. 4, Spring 1983. On parts of the SIOP organization, there is an official history paper prepared by the History and Research Division, Headquarters, Strategic Air Command, *History of the Joint Strategic Target Planning Staff: Background and Preparation of SIOP-62,* but it is only 18 pages long. Air Force General Richard Ellis wrote a similarly flimsy historical account, 11 pages long, called *The Joint Strategic Planning Staff;* Ellis was the director of strategic target planning and the paper is available at Offutt Air Force Base. An article entitled "The Single Integrated Operational Plan," by Capt. Mark Mariska, U.S. Army, appeared in *Military Review,* March 1972; it is helpful for a basic understanding of the various groups involved in putting the plan together.

A basic text, which is indispensible at this point in the history of the SIOP, is Desmond Ball's, *Politics and Force Levels: The Strategic Missile Program of the Kennedy Administration,*

Berkeley/Los Angeles, University of California Press, 1980; the book is an excellent grounding in the weaponry, targeting methods, and politics of the war plan.

For this chapter we had many interviews with armed forces personnel, both on active duty and retired. We also interviewed the late George Kistiakowsky, President Eisenhower's science adviser, and his two colleagues, George Rathjens of MIT and Herbert "Pete" Scoville, about their trip to Offutt in November 1960. Kistiakowsky's diary, *A Scientist at the White House*, Cambridge, Mass., Harvard University Press, 1976, has an account of the trip.

6: The Wimex

The best written sources on Wimex are congressional hearings and reports. They start in the early 1970s with three reports entitled, "Review of Defense Worldwide Communications Phase I" (10 May 1971), ". . . Phase II" (12 October 1972), and ". . . Phase III" (7 February 1975), by the Armed Services Investigating Subcommittee of the House of Representatives. Next is a series of reports from the General Accounting Office evaluating the purchase of the Honeywell computers: GAO *Report to Congress: NORAD's Information Processing Improvement Program—Will It Enhance Mission Capability?* LCD-78-1171, 21 September 1978; GAO *Report to Congress: The Worldwide Military Command and Control System—Major Changes Needed in Its Automated Data Processing Management and Direction*, LCD-80-22, 14 December 1979; GAO *Report to Congress: The WWMCCS—Evaluation of Vendor and Department of Defense Comments*, LCD-80-22A, 30 June 1980; GAO *Report to Congress: The WWMCCS—Problems in Information Resource Management*, MASAD-82-2, 19 October 1981.

The Carter administration set up their own inquiry into Wimex problems: *President's Reorganization Project*, 25 October 1978, Executive Office of the President; E.L. Dreeman, *Leader National Security Team Federal Data Processing Reorganization Project*, Office of Management and Budget, 1978.

A bipartisan Senate committee investigated the NORAD alerts in: *Recent False Alerts from the Nation's Missile Attack Warning System,* Report of Sen. Gary Hart and Sen. Barry Goldwater to the Committee on Armed Services, 9 October 1980. The House inquiry resulted in: *Failures of the North American Aerospace Defense Command's (NORAD) Attack Warning System,* Subcommittee of the Committee on Government Operations, House of Representatives, 19 and 20 May 1981. A third report from the House is entitled: NORAD *Computer Systems Are Dangerously Obsolete,* 23rd Report by the Committee on Government Operations, 8 March 1982.

Many newspaper and magazine articles were written about the false alerts. Among them are: "Foul-ups Beset U.S. Computer Defense System," *Baltimore Sun,* 28 October 1979; "False Alarm," *Norfolk Virginian Pilot,* 8 June 1980; "Not the Slightest Danger of War Being Triggered by Mistake: U.S. Alert a Defensive Mechanism," parliamentary report in *The Times,* London, 9 June 1980; two articles by Joseph Albright in the *Atlanta Constitution,* "Nuclear War Was Only a Moment Away," 13 June 1980, and "On Alert for Missile Attack: SAC Team Faces Another Threat—Computer Error," 16 June 1980, p. 1.

Two general articles about Wimex: James North, "Hello Central, Get Me NATO: The Computer That Can't," *Washington Monthly,* July/August 1979; replied to by Perry Nuhn, "WWMCCS and the Computer That Can," *Parameters, Journal of the U.S. Army War College,* September 1980.

A general Pentagon view of Wimex is found in the Department of Defense's fact sheets and in: Lt. Gen. Lee Paschall, "WWMCCS—Nerve Center of U.S. C³," *Air Force Magazine,* July 1973; John Fialka, "The Pentagon's Exercise, Proud Spirit: Little Cause for Pride," *Parameters, Journal of the U.S. Army War College,* March 1981.

John Bradley's story is told in: Rhonda Brown and Paul Matteucci, "The High Cost of Whistleblowing," *Inquiry Magazine,* 1 September 1981. Bradley was also interviewed by us in April 1982.

Some references on David Packard: "A Very Rich Man at the Pentagon," *Business Week*, 11 January 1969, p. 82; *Current Biography*, June 1969, p. 3; Robert Keatley, "Industrialist Packard Looms Large in Role as Key Defense Aide," *Wall Street Journal*, 12 December 1969, p. 1; "Packard Quits Defense Post," *Sunday Star*, Washington, D.C., 12 December 1971; "Nuclear Command Weak, Packard Warns," *Evening Star*, Washington, D.C., 20 March 1972, p. 82.

7: The Silent Services

The basic source of information on the characteristics of nuclear weapons is the book by Thomas Cochran and William Arkin, *Nuclear Weapons Databook*, Cambridge, Mass., Ballinger, 1983. The evolution of the weapons programs is contained in U.S. Department of Defense *Annual Reports*, JCS historical material, and information in the National Archives. Very useful books are: Desmond Ball, *Politics and Force Levels: The Strategic Missile Program of the Kennedy Administration*, Berkeley/Los Angeles, University of California Press, 1980; Edmund Beard, *Developing the ICBM*, New York, Columbia University Press, 1976; Strategic Air Command, *Development of the Strategic Air Command*, Office of the Historian, annually updated history of SAC, Offutt Air Force Base, Omaha, Neb.

A good overview of nuclear weapons issues and new weapons programs is the article by Deborah M. Kyle and Deborah G. Meyer, "SAC: Facing Up to Strategic Realities: Changing Perceptions, New Directions," *Armed Forces Journal International*, September 1981.

On nuclear weapons release and submarines, see: Phil Stanford, "Nuclear Missile Submarines and Nuclear Strategy," in David Johnson and Barry Schneider, eds., *Current Issues in U.S. Defense Policy*, New York, Praeger, 1976; U.S. Navy, Strategic Systems Project Office, *Fleet Ballistic Submarine Facts, 1981;* Jim Bencivenga, "Aboard a Nuclear Sub," *Christian Science Monitor*, 14 October 1982; Thomas S. Burns, *The Secret War for the Ocean Depths,* New York, Rawson Associates, 1978; "Trident Missile Capabilities," *Aviation Week & Space Technology,* 16 June 1980.

8: SIOP-5

The Big Stick war game is described in a series of publications from the U.S. Air Force Air Command and Staff College, Maxwell Air Force Base, Montgomery, Alabama. They are: *Big Stick, Instructions and Planning Guide,* January 1982; *Strategic Plans and Operations, Tailored Instructional Program,* March 1982; *Warfare Studies, Phase 2, Strategic Planning and Operations,* February/March 1982. Also from the U.S. Air Force Air Command and Staff College: *Readings and Seminars,* Vol. 10, January 1982.

Several papers and articles on PD-59 include: Desmond Ball, "Counterforce Targeting: How New? How Viable?" *Pacific Defense Reporter,* May 1981 (also in *Arms Control Today,* Washington, D.C., Arms Control Association, Vol. II, No. 2, February 1981); Desmond Ball, *Development in U.S. Strategic Nuclear Policy under the Carter Administration,* ACIS Working Paper No. 12, February 1980, Los Angeles, University of California, Center for International and Strategic Studies; Louis Renee Beres, "Tilting toward Thanatos: America's Countervailing Nuclear Strategy," *World Politics,* Vol. 34, No. 1, October 1981, pp. 25–46; Louis Renee Beres, "Presidential Directive 59: A Critical Assessment," *Parameters, Journal of the U.S. Army War College,* Vol. 11, No. 1, March 1981; Harold Brown, "A Countervailing Strategy," remarks delivered at Naval War College, Newport, R. I., 20 August 1980; Richard Burt, "The New Strategy for Nuclear War: How It Evolved," *New York Times,* 13 August 1980, p. 3; Richard Foster, "On Prolonged Nuclear War," *International Security Review,* Vol. 6, No. 4, Winter 1981–82, pp. 497–518; Leon Goure, "The U.S. Countervailing Strategy in Soviet Perception," *Strategic Review,* Fall 1981, pp. 51–64; Drew Middleton, "SAC Chief Is Critical of U.S. Nuclear War Plan," *New York Times,* 7 September 1980; Walter Slocombe, "The

Countervailing Strategy," *International Security*, Spring 1981, Vol. 5, No. 4, pp. 18–27.

On targeting the Soviet Union: Desmond Ball, *Issues in Strategic Nuclear Targeting: Target Selection and Rates of Fire*, Canberra, Australian National University, Strategic and Defence Studies Centre, prepared for 1982 Annual Meeting of the American Political Science Association, 2–5 September 1982; Colin Gray, "Targeting Problems for Central War," *Naval War College Review*, January/February 1980, p. 3; Jeffrey Richelson, "The Dilemmas of Counterpower Targeting," *Comparative Strategy*, Vol. 2, No. 3, 1980.

General accounts useful for interpreting the successive American strategic doctrines: Desmond Ball, *Politics and Force Levels: The Strategic Missile Program of the Kennedy Administration*, Berkeley/Los Angeles, University of California Press, 1980; Jimmy Carter, *Keeping Faith: Memoirs of a President*, New York, Bantam Books, 1982; Lynn Ethridge Davis, "Limited Nuclear Options: Deterrence and the New American Doctrine," *Adelphi Papers*, No. 21, London, International Institute for Strategic Studies; Lawrence Freedman, *Evolution of Strategic Thought*, London, Macmillan, 1982; Thomas Powers, "Choosing a Strategy for World War Three," *Atlantic Monthly*, November 1982, p. 82; Jerrold Schecter and Leona Schecter, "The War Planners," *Esquire*, January 1983, pp. 63–73.

On Soviet strategic doctrine: John Prados, *The Soviet Estimate: U.S. Intelligence Analysis and Russian Military Strength*, New York, Dial Press, 1982; William Lee, "Soviet Targeting Strategy and SALT," *Air Force Magazine*, September 1978.

9: Who's Minding the Store?

Numerous newspaper articles between 30 March and 5 April 1981 discussed the Reagan assassination attempt. The conflict between the U.S. Constitution and the National Command Authority was authoritatively discussed in far fewer reports, see: Mark M. Lowenthal, *National Security Policy: Conflicts over Control*, Congressional Research Service, Library of Congress,

18 May 1981; I.M. Destler, "National Security Advice to U.S. Presidents: Some Lessons from Thirty Years," *World Politics,* January 1977; numerous articles in *Presidential Studies Quarterly;* U.S. Congress, *Authority to Order the Use of Nuclear Weapons,* Report Prepared for the Subcommittee on International Security, House Committee on International Relations, 1 December 1975.

The National Command Authority and the National Military Command System are defined and discussed in: "Establishment of the National Communications System," White House Memorandum, 21 August 1963; of "World-Wide Military Command and Control System," U.S. Department of Defense Directive 5100.30, 2 December 1971; "National Communications System, Organization and Functions," June 1982. One of the best examinations of presidential control of nuclear weapons is: U.S. Congress, Committee on International Relations, *First Use of Nuclear Weapons: Preserving Responsible Control,* Hearings before the Subcommittee on International Security, House of Representitives, 1976.

Discussions of c^3 support to the president are contained in three sets of presentations and papers given at special c^3I seminars: *Electronics Systems Division,* Mitre Corporation; *National Security Issues 1981 Symposium: Strategic Nuclear Policies, Weapons, and the c^3 Connection,* Conference Report, 13–14 October 1981; *Seminar on Command, Control, Communications, and Intelligence,* Cambridge, Mass., Harvard University, transcript, Center for Information Policy Research, Spring 1980 and Spring 1981 (two volumes). Benjamin F. Schemmer, in "Who Would Start the War? A Civilian? The Military Advisor? Will It Be a Woman?" *Armed Forces Journal International,* December 1981, shrewdly examines nuclear war games and decision-making.

On the airborne command post support to the president, see: Capt. Katie Cutler, "Inside the Looking Glass," *Airman,* September 1982; Maureen Santini, "Reagan Gets His First Ride Aboard 'Doomsday Plane,' " *Philadelphia Inquirer,* 16 November 1981; Jam. Arvid P. Pederson, "Advanced Airborne Com-

mand Post: A Case Study," Air Command and Staff College
Student Report, Maxwell Air Force Base, Alabama, 1982.

One book that takes an alarmist view of presidential procedures is that by Bill Gulley and Mary Ellen Reese, *Breaking
Cover,* New York, Warner Books, 1980; the book, however, does
not give any plausible program for alleviating the insurmount-
able problems it identifies. Three new studies examine surprise
attack, presidential decision-making, and C^3I in the context of
new weapons technologies: Jack H. Nunn, *The Soviet First
Strike Threat: The U.S. Perspective,* New York, Praeger, 1982;
Richard K. Betts, *Surprise Attack,* Washington, D.C., Brookings
Institution, 1982; Daniel Frei, *Risks of Unintentional Nuclear
War,* London, Croom Helm, 1983. Finally, two important articles directly discuss the concept of "launch on warning": Rich-
ard L. Garwin, "Launch under Attack to Redress Minuteman
Vulnerability?" *International Security,* Winter 1979/80;
"Launch under Attack," in *MX Missile Basing,* 1982, available
from the Office of Technology Assessment, U.S. Congress,

10: Decapitation

The basic source for understanding the present decapitation
argument and the connection with nuclear weapons policy is
the excellent Desmond Ball monograph, "Can Nuclear War Be
Controlled," *Adelphi Papers,* No. 169, London, International
Institute for Strategic Studies, 1981.

A number of sources give a good overview of the evolution
of military communications and C^3I, other than the Department of Defense annual reports and Mitre Corporation reports
already mentioned. Some of these sources include: U.S. Army
Communications Command, *History of the United States Army
Communications Command from Origin through 1976,* Fort
Huachuca, Ariz., December 1977; U.S. Army Communications
Command, *Introduction to Satellite Communications,* Huachuca, Ariz., 15 April 1974; U.S. Air Force Communications
Command, "AACS, AFCS, AFCC, *1938–1981, Providing the Reins
of Command,*" Office of History, Scott Air Force Base, Illinois,

1981; Richard E. Fitts, *The Strategy of Electromagnetic Conflict*, Los Altos, Calif., Peninsula, 1980; Air University, *Space Handbook*, Maxwell Air Force Base, Alabama, August 1977.

One of the first comprehensive reports of the problems of defense communications and C³I was: U.S. Congress, Committee on Armed Services, House of Representatives, *Review of Department of Defense Worldwide Communications, Phase I*, Report of the Armed Services Investigating Subcommittee, 10 May 1971, After this report, a number of significant reports and articles further developed the issue of a C³I problem: U.S. Congress, Committee on Armed Services, House of Representatives, *Review of Department of Defense Command, Control and Communications System and Facilities*, Report by the Command, Control and Communications Panel, Nigel Calder, "The Headless Dragon," in *Nuclear Nightmares*, New York, Viking, 1980; Congressional Budget Office, *Strategic Command, Control, and Communications: Alternative Approaches for Modernization*, October 1981; John D. Steinbruner, "Nuclear Decapitation," *Foreign Policy*, Winter 1981–82; "Command, Control, and Communications (C³)," in MX *Missile Basing*, 1982, available from the Office of Technology Assessment,

On submarine communications, see: Vice Admiral Sir Arthur Hezlet, *Electronics and Sea Power*, New York, Stein and Day, 1975; Lowell L. Lessig and Victor L. Strite, *The ELF Odyssey: National Security versus Environmental Protection*, Boulder, Colo., Westview, 1980; U.S. General Accounting Office, *An Unclassified Version of a Classified Report Entitled "The Navy's Strategic Communications Systems—Need for Management Attention and Decisionmaking,"* 2 May 1979. The Navy also has produced a lot of material justifying the ELF program and bemoaning the fragility of submarine links.

Some more recent articles that address the connections between C³I and the new nuclear strategy include: U.S. Department of Defense, *C³I Program Management Structure and Major Programs*, 10 December 1980, declassified; Jeffrey Richelson, *PD-59 and the Reagan Strategic Program*, Center for International and Strategic Affairs, UCLA, August 1982; Charles A.

Zraket, "Technological Infrastructure for Enduring C^3I Systems," Mitre Corporation briefing, 13 October 1981; "Remarks at Aspen Institute Conference on Security and Arms Control— July 1981, PD-59 and C^3I," Mitre Corporation, July 1981.

Epilogue: Degrading Gracefully

Articles, papers, and reports on the Reagan plan include: *Collection of Recent Reagan Administration References to Nuclear War-Fighting and Winning,* Washington, D.C., Center for Defense Information, January 1982; Hans Bethe and Kurt Gottfried, "Assessing Reagan's Doomsday Scenarios," *New York Times,* 11 April 1982; "General Jones Rebutts Foes of A-Strategy," Associated Press interview, 28 April 1982; "Weinberger Denies U.S. Plans for 'Protracted War,'" *New York Times,* 21 June 1982, p. 5; Robert Scheer, "Pentagon Plan Aims at Victory in Nuclear War," *Los Angeles Times,* 15 August 1982, p. 1; Caspar Weinberger, Letter to foreign editors on protracted nuclear war, 23 August 1982; Richard Halloran, "Weinberger Angered by Report on War Strategy," *New York Times,* 24 August 1982; Edgar Prina, "New Defense Guidance Services to 'Get in Step,'" *Sea Power,* August 1982, pp. 43–44, 48, 51; Jerrold Schecter and Leona Schecter, "The War Planners," *Esquire,* January 1983; Robert Scheer, *With Enough Shovels: Reagan, Bush and Nuclear War,* New York, Random House, 1981.

On the future of nuclear deterrence: "The Future of Strategic Deterrence," Parts I and II, *Adelphi Papers,* Nos. 160 and 161, London, International Institute for Strategic Studies, 1980.

Index